the Model
Work Health
and Safety Act

DISCLAIMER

Understanding the Model Work Health and Safety Act

a Wolters Kluwer business

Barry Sherriff
Michael Tooma

CCH AUSTRALIA LIMITED
GPO Box 4072, Sydney, NSW 2001

Head Office North Ryde
Phone: (02) 9857 1300 Fax: (02) 9857 1600

Customer Support
Phone: 1 300 300 224 Fax: 1 300 306 224
www.cch.com.au

Book Code: 39098A

ABOUT CCH AUSTRALIA LIMITED

CCH Australia is a leading provider of accurate, authoritative and timely information services for professionals. Our position as the 'professional's first choice' is built on the delivery of expert information that is relevant, comprehensive and easy to use.

We are a member of the Wolters Kluwer group, a leading global information services provider with a presence in more than 25 countries in Europe, North America and Asia Pacific.

CCH – *The Professional's First Choice.*

Enquiries are welcome on **1300 300 224**

Cataloguing-in-Publication Data available through the National Library of Australia.

ISBN: 978 1 921593 72 7

Reprinted .... June 2010
Reprinted .... February 2011
© 2010 CCH Australia Limited

Printed in Australia by McPherson's Printing Group

ABOUT THE AUTHORS

Michael Tooma is an Adjunct Professor of Law at Edith Cowan University, Senior Visiting Fellow of the School of Law at the University of New South Wales, and Partner of Norton Rose Australia. Michael heads up Norton Rose's OHS practice.

Michael is the author of several books on OHS law including: the plain English guide to OHS law, *The Hands On Guide: OHS Legal Guide*, published by CCH; the ground-breaking text, *Safety, Security, Health and Environment Law*, published by Federation Press; and the renowned series of annotated legislation on the New South Wales and Victorian OHS legislation, *Tooma's Annotated Occupational Health and Safety Act*, published by Thomson Reuters.

Michael is the leading commentator on OHS legislative developments, regularly providing print, radio and television media interviews on developments in the law. From the harmonisation of OHS laws, to the threat of a swine flu outbreak, to the regulation of nanotechnology, to commentary on the implications of the latest court decisions, Michael's authoritative but plain-speaking explanations of complex issues have made him a sought-after commentator on OHS issues.

Michael was named in the OHS category in the Best Lawyers Australia list for 2010.

Barry Sherriff is an OHS Partner of Norton Rose Australia. Barry provides advice and proactive strategies for compliance and risk management in OHS and associated areas of WorkCover issues, employment and discrimination. He represents clients across industries including finance, transport, manufacturing, mining and government. His experience has included the development and review of risk management and OHS strategies and corporate governance structures and procedures.

Barry was a member of the Panel that made recommendations to Federal, State and Territory governments on the structure and content of a model OHS Act to be adopted in all jurisdictions. The model Work Health and Safety Act, approved by the Workplace Relations Ministers' Council in December 2009, closely follows the recommendations of the Panel.

Barry is an acknowledged thought leader in OHS, regularly speaking at conferences and contributing to OHS-specific and general publications. Among his various publications, Barry has authored *OHS in Practice — A Guide to Legislation in Victoria*, published by Anstat in 2005. He is a contributor to the CCH *Master OHS and Environment Guide*.

Barry is an Honorary Fellow of the Safety Institute of Australia and is the OHS Coordinator of the Property Council of Australia. He is a member of the National Employers' OHS Consultative Forum and the WorkSafe Victoria Stakeholder Reference Group.

Barry was named in the Labour and Employment category in the Best Lawyers Australia list in 2008 and 2009.

CONTENTS

About the authors... v

Preface ix

Chapter 1   The path to harmonisation 1

Chapter 2   Primary duties of care 15

Chapter 3   Officers' duty of care... 29

Chapter 4   Rights and duties of workers and other people at
             workplaces... 49

Chapter 5   Public sector obligations 61

Chapter 6   Workplace participation and protection..................... 67

Chapter 7   Enforcement and compliance................................... 95

Index.. 113

CCH ACKNOWLEDGMENTS

CCH Australia Ltd wishes to thank the following team members who contributed to this publication:

Managing Director
Staffan Wensing

Publishing Director
Matthew Sullivan

Editor-in-Chief
John Stafford

Portfolio Projects Manager
Kate Aylett-Graham

Editor
Deborah Powell

Indexing
Graham Clayton

Production
Lata Prabakaran

Marketing
Simon Wilkins — Director of Sales and Marketing
Frederik Ericson — Marketing Project Manager
Antonina Cocilovo — Marketing Executive
Mathias Johansson — Designer

PREFACE

The model Work Health and Safety Act represents the most significant reform to occupational health and safety laws in Australia since the initial introduction of Robens-style legislation over thirty years ago.

While the model laws emanated from a process of harmonisation of existing State and Territory-based OHS laws, the final outcome goes well beyond that.

The model laws introduce new concepts of duty holders, broader approaches to workplace participation and safety corporate governance, and higher penalties. These changes put safety at the forefront of corporate decision-making. The changes also reflect the need for the law to accommodate changes in the way in which work is arranged. The laws ensure that every person involved in work being done behaves in the interests of health and safety, and that no worker lacks the protection of OHS laws.

The laws are titled "work health and safety". But it would be a mistake to assume that the new laws are limited to the workplace, or indeed that the concept of a workplace is at all a critical concept to the operation of the laws. The laws apply to work wherever it is done as part of a business, that is, they apply as much to the home as they do to the workplace, as much to a road, an airport lounge, a hotel room, a shopping centre as they do to a factory, a shop or an office. Nor is the concept of a worker, broad as it is, a lynchpin to the operation of the legislation. The laws apply as much to a pedestrian as they do to labourers in a factory, as much to a customer in a shopping centre as they do to a shop assistant in a store. These are health and safety laws with broad, all-encompassing reach which seek to regulate safety standards across all business activities.

This book attempts to explain the model laws in a simple and concise manner. It is not intended as a detailed commentary but, rather, a plain English explanation of the laws for everyday users. In that regard, it is aimed primarily at safety practitioners and managers in both the private and public sector.

The book deals with each of the key elements of the laws in the context of the overall system envisaged by the model laws. This is important because the discussion and recommendations of the National OHS Review Panel make it clear that each element of the laws is part of an integrated system. Each element supports, or is interdependent on, other elements.

The authors would like to thank Deborah Powell from CCH for her skilful editing of this book under tight time constraints. They would also like to thank Kate Graham from CCH for her enthusiastic commitment to the book from its inception.

On a personal level, the authors would each like to thank their families for their support. Barry would like to thank his wife Jackie for her good spirits and encouragement which helped to sustain him not only during the writing of this book, but also throughout his career and his role on the National OHS Review Panel. Michael would like to thank his wife Rachel for her unwavering support and encouragement, and his daughter Kaitlyn for her patience with her father. Michael would like to dedicate this book to the memory of his mother, Viviane.

Barry Sherriff

Michael Tooma

March 2010

CHAPTER 1

THE PATH TO HARMONISATION

The model Work Health and Safety Act (model WHS Act) will provide a high level of uniformity in work health and safety legislation throughout Australia as a result of its enactment by the Commonwealth Parliament and each of the State and Territory parliaments. It is useful to look at the reasons for the harmonisation of work health and safety laws in Australia, and the process by which this has been achieved, in order to provide a context for a consideration of the detail of the model laws and the changes that will be effected by them. This discussion also aids an understanding of the need for developing the law to meet changing work arrangements and environments.

A brief history of work health and safety laws in Australia[1]

The regulation of work health and safety in Australia has been heavily influenced by the development of the law in the United Kingdom. Until the latter part of the 20th century, work health and safety laws were focused on specific industries, workplaces and risks. Different and subject matter-specific laws were enacted for factories, mines, railways and machinery. Those laws were directed at specific risks and were prescriptive in nature.

The most significant event in the development and "modernisation" of work health and safety regulation in the UK and Australia was the delivery in 1972 of the *Report of the Committee on Safety and Health at Work* (referred to as the Robens Report, the Committee having been chaired by Lord Robens). The Robens Report identified numerous deficiencies in, and limitations of, the existing laws. The laws were considered to be:

- uncoordinated, complex and confusing;
- too detailed and prescriptive to be applicable across all workplaces;
- inflexible and unable to keep pace with technological, social and economic change;

---

1 This section is not intended to provide a comprehensive summary of the development of work health and safety laws in Australia. It provides a context for the model WHS Act. For further information on the historical development of the law in Australia, see Johnstone, R, *Occupational health and safety law and policy*, Sydney, Law Book Company, 2004, ch 2; Tooma, M, *Safety, security, health and environment law*, Sydney, Federation Press, 2008, pp 4–12; and Creighton, WB and Rozen, P, *Occupational health and safety law in Victoria*, Sydney, Federation Press, 1997, pp 2–11.

- activity rather than outcome-focused (compliance would not necessarily mean effective management of risks); and
- ineffective in enforcing proper conduct by providing for maximum penalties for breaches that were so low as to have little or no deterrent effect.

The regulatory model recommended in the Robens Report has been adopted in the UK and Australia, and has addressed many of these deficiencies. In place of prescriptive requirements, the Robens model requires that laws set performance-based or outcome-focused standards (that is, duties to achieve safe outcomes). Rather than directing specific activities, the Robens model requires duty holders (those involved in the undertaking of work and providing the means for work to be undertaken) to achieve safe outcomes by the means which can be adopted, and are most appropriately adopted, in the circumstances of the particular business or work activities. Inconsistency, complexity and confusion through the proliferation of health and safety-related laws were addressed by enacting a single piece of legislation directed at health and safety. The obligations of all of the parties involved in work became clearer, and penalties were substantially increased. The Robens model also addressed the practical requirements for achieving health and safety outcomes in specific workplaces. The report recommended the involvement and engagement of employers and employees in determining what ought to be done for health and safety through workplace consultation requirements.

The Robens model was adopted in the UK in the *Health and Safety at Work etc. Act 1974*. The model was progressively adopted throughout Australia from 1983.[2]

The laws relating to work health and safety in Australia remain consistent with the Robens model. The model WHS Act will also be consistent with that model, but will build on it in significant ways.

Ongoing reviews of the legislation

Governments and regulators in each of the Australian jurisdictions have, over the last decade or so, appreciated that the then existing regulatory regime failed to adequately reduce the unacceptably high levels of death and injury in Australian workplaces. The governments and regulators undertook reviews of the work health and safety laws that resulted in amendments to the legislation and regulations. Not all of the recommendations from the reviews and resultant reports were adopted, and while there was some commonality in the recommendations in the various reviews, different aspects of the recommendations were adopted in the jurisdictions,

---

2 New South Wales was the first State to adopt the Robens model in 1983, followed quickly by Western Australia in 1984, Victoria in 1985, and South Australia in 1986.

and in different ways. This has resulted in the laws (which did not all uniformly adopt the Robens model) moving away from each other.

Jurisdictional "uniqueness"

A common reason given for a State or Territory government making changes to what would otherwise be uniform laws, or adding further obligations or requirements to its laws, has been that the commercial or industrial environment in the jurisdiction is so different as to need special treatment. It has been said that jurisdictions that focus more heavily on mining, agriculture, tourism, manufacturing or the provision of services need laws that deal with the special requirements presented by that focus. This has been particularly so with regard to the introduction of regulations.

The benefits of harmonising work health and safety laws

In 1995, the Industry Commission noted that:

> "Nationally uniform OHS standards have been a goal since the creation of the National Occupational Health and Safety Commission (NOHSC) in 1984. However, NOHSC made little progress towards that goal until November 1991 when Heads of Government agreed to implement nationally uniform standards through NOHSC by the end of 1993."[3]

While progress was made through the development of regulations in seven key areas,[4] the regulations were not adopted uniformly by the jurisdictions, and it took almost a decade before all of the jurisdictions adopted all of the regulations.

The need for harmonisation of work health and safety laws was recognised by the Industry Commission, which noted:

> "Jurisdictions place different obligations on employers, employees and suppliers. Some exposure limits — such as for noise and asbestos — differ as do some rules for hazardous plant, equipment and work processes. There are differences in enforcement. Such differences mean there are different levels of protection for workers doing the same job in the various jurisdictions — this is inequitable.

---

3   Industry Commission, *Work health and safety: enquiry into occupational health and safety*, Canberra, Commonwealth of Australia, 1995, p xxvii.
4   Asbestos, noise, manual handling, lead, plant, certification of users of plant, and hazardous substances.

Employers with operations in more than one state have to work with multiple OHS regimes. This means additional costs whenever systems of work are changed or staff are moved; they also raise the cost of their internal monitoring of compliance."[5]

The Productivity Commission further considered the desirability of harmonisation in 2004 in its report, *National Workers' Compensation and Occupational Health and Safety Frameworks.*[6]

A critical point in the activities leading to the model WHS Act was the Productivity Commission's 2006 report, *Rethinking Regulation: Report of the Taskforce on Reducing Regulatory Burdens on Business.*[7] While that report dealt with numerous areas, it dealt specifically with OHS, and recommended that:

"COAG [Council of Australian Governments] should implement nationally consistent standards for occupational health and safety (OH&S) and apply a test whereby jurisdictions must demonstrate a net public benefit if they want to vary a national OH&S standard or code to suit local conditions."[8]

Following that recommendation, COAG directed the Workplace Relations Ministers' Council (WRMC) to develop strategies to improve the implementation and uptake of national OHS standards through various means, including identifying priority areas that should be harmonised in the principal OHS Acts in each State and Territory.[9]

A series of reports produced by the WRMC has identified current differences between the regulatory regimes and their performance.[10]

The Australian Safety and Compensation Council (ASCC) was established by the WRMC in 2005 to coordinate national OHS activities and promote national OHS consistency.

---

5   Industry Commission, op cit, p xxv.
6   Productivity Commission, *National workers' compensation and occupational health and safety frameworks*, Canberra, Commonwealth of Australia, 2004.
7   Productivity Commission, *Rethinking regulation: report of the taskforce on reducing regulatory burdens on business*, Canberra, Commonwealth of Australia, 2006.
8   Ibid, recommendation 4.26.
9   Commonwealth of Australia, *Rethinking regulation: report of the taskforce on reducing regulatory burdens on business — Australian Government's response*, Canberra, Commonwealth of Australia, 2006, p 14.
10   See, for example, Workplace Relations Ministers' Council, *Comparative performance monitoring report: comparison of occupational health and safety and workers' compensation schemes in Australia and New Zealand* (8th ed), Canberra, WRMC, 2006; and Workplace Relations Ministers' Council, *Comparison of occupational health and safety arrangements in Australia and New Zealand* (4th ed), Canberra, WRMC, 2004.

The States and Territories took various steps to progress the harmonisation of OHS regulation, for example, by forming the Council for the Australian Federation in October 2006, and the Eastern Seaboard Alliance (comprising Queensland, New South Wales and Victoria) in 2006.

The social partners through the Australian Council of Trade Unions and the National Employers Occupational Health and Safety Consultative Forum contributed to the harmonisation endeavours of these various bodies.

The national OHS review

On 1 February 2008, the WRMC agreed that the use of model legislation is the most effective way to achieve harmonisation of OHS laws. Accordingly, the WRMC decided to initiate a review of the existing laws in order to develop model legislation. Following that decision, terms of reference for the review were agreed by the WRMC[11] and, in April 2008, a panel of three people was established to undertake the review.[12]

The Panel was required by the Terms of Reference to:

- examine the principal OHS legislation of each jurisdiction to identify areas of best practice, common practice and inconsistency;
- take into account relevant work that had already been undertaken in various reviews (including international developments);
- take into account the changing nature of work and employment arrangements;
- consult broadly, including inviting submissions from the public and other stakeholders; and
- make recommendations on the optimal structure and content of a model OHS Act that promotes safe workplaces, increases certainty for duty holders, reduces compliance costs for business, and provides greater clarity for regulators without compromising safety outcomes.

In May 2008, the Panel produced an Issues Paper inviting submissions on 152 questions raised on the various aspects of OHS regulation. The Panel received 242 written submissions,[13] providing it with the views of stakeholders on important issues and references to relevant research material.

---

11   Workplace Relations Ministers' Council, *National review into model occupational health and safety laws: first report to the Workplace Relations Ministers' Council* (First Report), Canberra, WRMC, October 2008, Terms of Reference, pp ii–v.

12   Mr Robin Stewart-Crompton (chair), and Mr Barry Sherriff and Ms Stephanie Mayman (members).

13   The submissions can be found at www.nationalohsreview.gov.au/ohs/PublicSubmissions.

The submissions demonstrated a significant degree of consistency in many of the key areas, but there was considerable disparity of views on some issues, including:

- how the laws could accommodate changes in work arrangements;
- whether "reasonably practicable" should be a qualifier within the duties of care, or part of a defence to a prosecution for a breach identified by a finding of risk, that is, who should bear the burden of proof in a prosecution;
- whether reasonably practicable should be defined, and how;
- whether risk management principles should be mandated in the legislation;
- whether "control" should be an element, or a qualifier, of duties of care and, if so, whether control should be defined;
- whether "officers" should have a duty of care, the substance of such a duty, and who should be an officer for that purpose;
- whether offences should give rise to civil or criminal penalties, or both;
- whether the laws should provide for any defences and, if so, what those defences should be;
- the roles and powers of health and safety representatives;
- the role of unions in workplace consultation, the right of entry of unions to a workplace, and whether unions should be able to investigate and prosecute offences;
- the role of the regulator, and the powers to be exercised by the regulator and inspectors; and
- the level of penalties.

The Panel consulted broadly with a wide range of stakeholders in all States and Territories. Research was undertaken and consideration given to the reports of recent reviews of OHS laws in Australia, the characteristics and elements of overseas legislation and regulatory systems, international trends, academic literature and other source material.[14]

As is evident from the submissions, the representatives of workers were concerned to ensure unions were provided with broad rights of entry to workplaces and involvement in work health and safety matters, and would have extensive powers (including the power to prosecute). They also submitted that worker representatives should have broad investigative and coercive powers. Worker representatives favoured the onus of proof in a prosecution being on the defendant, with the standard of

---

14   Referred to throughout the two reports that the Panel produced.

reasonably practicable being part of a defence, not a qualifier of a duty of care. They also promoted substantially increased penalties.[15]

Those who made submissions on behalf of industry associations and organisations tended to want to limit the roles and powers of worker representatives, although a number saw benefits to their involvement — so long as safeguards were provided. They overwhelmingly favoured the inclusion of reasonably practicable as a qualifier of duties of care, with the burden of proof being borne by the prosecution. Union rights to prosecute were strongly opposed. Opinions were divided among this group of stakeholders on whether offences should be criminal or civil in nature, and on the level of penalties.

In accordance with the Terms of Reference, the Panel produced two reports (one in October 2008 and one in January 2009).[16]

The Panel made the following recommendations with regard to the issues noted above:

- there should be a primary duty of care on a person conducting a business or an undertaking, rather than an employer (this is discussed further below and in chapter 2);
- reasonably practicable should be a qualifier of the primary duty of care (and subsets of the primary duty of care relating to specific activities of a person conducting a business or an undertaking), and should be defined;
- the prosecution should bear the burden of proving a failure by a duty holder to meet the standard of reasonably practicable (defences would not be required to duty of care offences);
- the application of risk management principles, while inherent in meeting the duties of care, should not be mandated as a process in the model WHS Act;
- control should not specifically be a qualifier of duties of care, or be included in the definition of reasonably practicable (to avoid undue focus on this element), but is recognised as an inherent consideration when determining what a duty holder is able to do and ought reasonably do;
- officers should have a positive duty of care, with the standard of conduct (due diligence) being clearly defined;

---

15 For example, the Construction, Forestry, Mining and Energy Union submitted that the maximum penalty for a duty of care breach by an employer should be at least $6m or a percentage of the annual turnover of the organisation.

16 Workplace Relations Ministers' Council, *National review into model occupational health and safety laws: first report to the Workplace Relations Ministers' Council* (First Report), Canberra, WRMC, October 2008; and WRMC, *National review into model occupational health and safety laws: second report to the Workplace Relations Ministers' Council* (Second Report), Canberra, WRMC, January 2009.

- duty of care breaches should be criminal offences, with criminal penalties applied;

- the regulator should have a primary role as an advisor (generally and on specific issues at a workplace), but should also be provided with broad enforcement powers;

- the importance of consultation between work participants should be recognised and supported through a broadening of consultation obligations;

- the elected health and safety representatives of workers should be given powers to issue notices and to direct that unsafe work ceases;

- unions should be given broader rights on entry (to inquire into breaches, and to consult and advise members or eligible workers), but should not be given the power to prosecute, which should be reserved to the State;

- protection against discrimination and coercion should be significantly enhanced to cover a broader range of people who participate in work health and safety roles and activities; and

- penalties should be increased to above the highest level currently applicable in Australia, but there should be a focus on alternative sentencing options as part of a process of graduated enforcement.

The Commonwealth of Australia and each of the States and Territories entered into the *Inter-governmental Agreement for Regulatory and Operational Reform in Occupational Health and Safety* on 3 July 2008 (the IGA).[17] Under the IGA, the governments agreed to a process by which model OHS legislation, supported by model OHS regulations and model codes of practice, would be developed to provide for the harmonisation of OHS laws (described in the IGA as uniform OHS legislation). The IGA also presented the means by which national uniformity of the OHS legislation would be maintained by providing for processes for the justification for and adoption of changes.

The decisions of the WRMC, the IGA and the review process provided a means by which the harmonisation of health and safety laws in Australia could occur — at a single point in time and within a relatively short space of time — and be sustained.

The WRMC considered the two reports of the Panel and, on 18 May 2009, made decisions on each of the 232 recommendations.[18] Following acceptance of over 90%

---

17   Commonwealth and States and Territories of Australia, *Inter-governmental agreement for regulatory and operational reform in occupational health and safety* (the IGA), Canberra, Commonwealth and States and Territories of Australia, 3 July 2008.

18   See *Communiqué from Australian, State, Territory and New Zealand Workplace Relations Ministers' Council*, 18 May 2009, and the accompanying WRMC response to recommendations of the national review into model OHS laws.

of the recommendations of the Panel (some with modifications), the WRMC asked the Safe Work Australia Council to develop the model OHS laws in accordance with the WRMC decisions on the Panel's recommendations.

The model WHS Act is the outcome of that process, including extensive stakeholder consultation following the release of an exposure draft bill for public consultation. The WRMC also asked the Safe Work Australia Council to develop model regulations and codes of practice to support the model Act — with that task being underway at the time of writing.

It is intended that the Parliament in each of the jurisdictions will enact the model WHS Act in mid-2011, for commencement by 1 January 2012. The jurisdictions are required by the IGA to "enact or otherwise give effect to their own laws that mirror the model laws as far as possible having regard to the drafting protocols in each jurisdiction".[19]

Achieving consistency and improvement in work health and safety regulation

The key drivers in developing model OHS laws were the achievement of equity between workers (providing the same rights and protections regardless of location or occupation) and the production of significant financial benefits for industry by reducing the regulatory burden.

The Terms of Reference for the Panel made it clear, however, that the process was designed to do more than merely produce uniform legislation and regulation. The Terms of Reference required the Panel to make recommendations on the optimal content of an OHS Act that "promotes safe workplaces, increases certainty for duty holders, reduces compliance costs for business and provides greater clarity for regulators without compromising safety outcomes".[20]

The Panel was required to take into account recommendations from recent reviews, international developments, and the changing nature of work and employment arrangements. The recommendations of the Panel and the resultant model laws are intended to not only provide for consistency in OHS laws throughout Australia, but to also improve the effectiveness of those laws. This is to be achieved by:

- more, and more explanatory, definitions of key terms;
- clearer and more explanatory language;

---

19   IGA, op cit, cl 5.1.7.
20   First Report, Terms of Reference, cl 11(e).

- less reliance on determining the legal status of the holder of a duty or obligation or those to whom the duties and obligations relate;

- enhancing provisions that assist work health and safety management, including consultation and the role of regulators and inspectors to provide guidance; and

- the use of graduated enforcement and various sentencing options to promote health and safety improvements.

Accommodating changed workplace arrangements

The Robens model of OHS legislation has served the UK and Australia well for over thirty years. Many aspects of the Robens model remain valid, and the recommendations of the Panel and the model laws adopt a number of the fundamental concepts of the Robens model.

It must, however, be recognised that almost four decades have passed since the Robens Report, during which time there have been significant changes to the type of work which is undertaken, the means by which it is undertaken (for example, technological change), and the way in which it is undertaken (that is, changes in the way in which people are engaged to undertake work and are directed and supervised in that work).

The most common and traditional means by which work was arranged in the early 1970s was through the employment relationship. That relationship involved a high level of control and direction by the employer of the employees. That control and the implications of it for the safety of the employees was, for many decades, recognised by the common law imposing on an employer a non-delegable duty of care to its employees. The Robens Report accordingly used the employment relationship to determine the duties of care owed by those controlling or directing the work (the employer) to those undertaking the work (the employees). Associated obligations and the arrangements for workplace consultation on health and safety matters were also determined by reference to the employment relationship.

Since the Robens Report, alternatives to the employment relationship for the arrangement of work have become more diverse and more common. Those alternatives include contracting, labour hire, student placement, share farming, share fishing and similar arrangements, bartering for labour, and the use of volunteers.[21]

---

21   See ch 2 of the First Report (pp 12–15) on "Changes in the organisation of work" and the various references noted in the footnotes. See, also, the chapter by Johnstone, R, "Regulating occupational health and safety in a changing labour market" in Arup, C (ed), *Labour law and labour market regulation*, Sydney, Federation Press, 2006, pp 617–636.

Legislation and regulations based on the employment relationship accordingly do not clearly provide protection for all who are undertaking work, or require those who have the control and direction of work to take appropriate measures for the protection of the health and safety of all those who are working for them.

While there is broad coverage through the duties of care placed on employers in relation to the conduct of their business or undertaking, these do not direct the employer to the specific requirements that are stated to apply in relation to employees.

Another issue is that consultation obligations and rights in current legislation apply to employers and employees, thereby excluding those not involved in an employment relationship.

These limitations have, in part, been addressed in some OHS Acts, for example, by the deeming of contractors and their employees to be employees of the principal for some purposes.[22] However, the coverage afforded by deeming provisions such as these is limited by their terms. By specifying specific circumstances for their operation, the laws can encourage endeavours to avoid their application. It can be difficult to determine whether the law applies to specific circumstances. This can mean that a significant focus is determining whether someone has an obligation or not, rather than what they should do to protect the health and safety of those working for them.

There have also been significant changes in where work is done and the characteristics of those undertaking the work that are relevant to the effectiveness of work health and safety regulation and arrangements.[23] Workers gathering to work full time at a single workplace was the norm when the Robens Committee was making its recommendations. Working from home, at the workplaces of others, and travelling for work are now common. Workers are now regularly engaged for part-time work, casual work and contracting.[24] These factors can present challenges for the effective management of health and safety, by potentially limiting opportunities for consultation, training and risk assessments.

It is for these reasons that the WRMC wanted to make sure that the Panel and the model laws took into account the changing nature of workplace arrangements and endeavoured to broaden the coverage and operation of the legislation.

---

22 For example, *Occupational Health and Safety Act 2004* (Vic), s 21(3).

23 See the discussion on pp 14–17 of the First Report and the resources referred to in the footnotes.

24 The Productivity Commission noted, in its report *The role of non-traditional work in the Australian labour market* (2006), that there were approximately 843,900 independent contractors in 1998, representing over 10% of the workforce. The ABS *Year Book 2008* noted that the proportion of employed people who worked part time rose from 19% in 1986/87 to 28% in 2006/07.

Using enforcement to achieve better safety outcomes

The enforcement of work health and safety laws is important to the outcomes produced by the regulatory system. Laws should encourage performance and punish offenders, as is appropriate to support the objectives of the laws. Imprisonment and fines have traditionally been the most common (and, in many cases, exclusive) means of enforcing laws and punishing offenders. However, considerable work has been undertaken in recent decades on the effectiveness of these measures and on alternatives to imprisonment and fines that may better promote the objectives of the laws.

Work health and safety laws are directed at protecting the health and safety of people undertaking, or affected by the undertaking of, work. The enforcement of those laws, including the sentencing of offenders, should be directed at promoting this objective of the laws in a manner that is most appropriate to the circumstances. This has been the subject of significant discussion in recent reviews of OHS legislation in Australia, and was taken up by the Panel in chapter 12 of the First Report.

The model WHS Act includes various alternative sentencing options that are designed to produce optimal safety outcomes from the prosecution process (these are considered later in chapter 7). The model WHS Act also adopts the recommendations of the Panel for graduated enforcement of the law by providing advice and assistance, issuing coercive or prohibiting notices, agreeing to enforceable undertakings, and ultimately prosecution.[25]

How the model laws aim to improve health and safety regulation

In summary, the model laws will introduce a number of significant changes (which will be discussed further in later chapters), including:

1. a greater focus on assisting and promoting health and safety activities through:
   a. clearer language and improved definitions; and
   b. giving greater prominence to the duties of care and enabling processes (consultation, representation, issue resolution and regulator advice) by moving legal and enforcement provisions to the back of the model WHS Act;
2. moving away from the employment relationship and deeming provisions to determine who owes duties of care and who has obligations, ensuring broad coverage of the laws;

---

25   See ch 35, 36 and 39 of the Second Report.

3. enhanced protection against discrimination and coercion;

4. broadened rights for representation and rights of representatives, including broadened union rights of entry;

5. providing for and encouraging graduated enforcement, with alternative sentencing options for improvements in health and safety; and

6. significant increases in the maximum fines, and introducing categories of offence.

The process moving forward

Model regulations to support the model WHS Act are being drafted through a process involving the agency of Safe Work Australia, a tri-partite strategic issues group, and various tri-partite technical advisory groups. The regulations will be released for public comment late in 2010 (for a period of approximately four months). The regulations will be finalised following consideration of the comments received.

Codes of practice and guidance material are also being progressively developed, with the major focus on these documents being during 2011.

It is currently intended that the model WHS Act will be enacted in mid-2011, for commencement on 1 January 2012. The lag period from now until the enactment and commencement of the laws is to enable all of the parts to be introduced together, and for the model WHS Act to undergo any modifications that are necessary to accommodate jurisdictional drafting conventions or criminal justice requirements and any matters raised during the development of the regulations. It is intended that any modifications to the model WHS Act will be to the technical wording, with the policy positions, duties, obligations and rights having been settled.

CHAPTER 2

PRIMARY DUTIES OF CARE

The model Work Health and Safety Act (model WHS Act) provides for various parties who are involved in, or contribute to, the undertaking of work to owe duties of care to those who are affected by the work being undertaken. The various duties of care are found in Divisions 2, 3 and 4 of Part 2 of the model WHS Act.

The respective roles of those involved in activities associated with the conduct of work, why they each therefore have a duty of care, and the standard that they are to meet are represented in the following diagram.[1]

Relationship between recommended duties of care

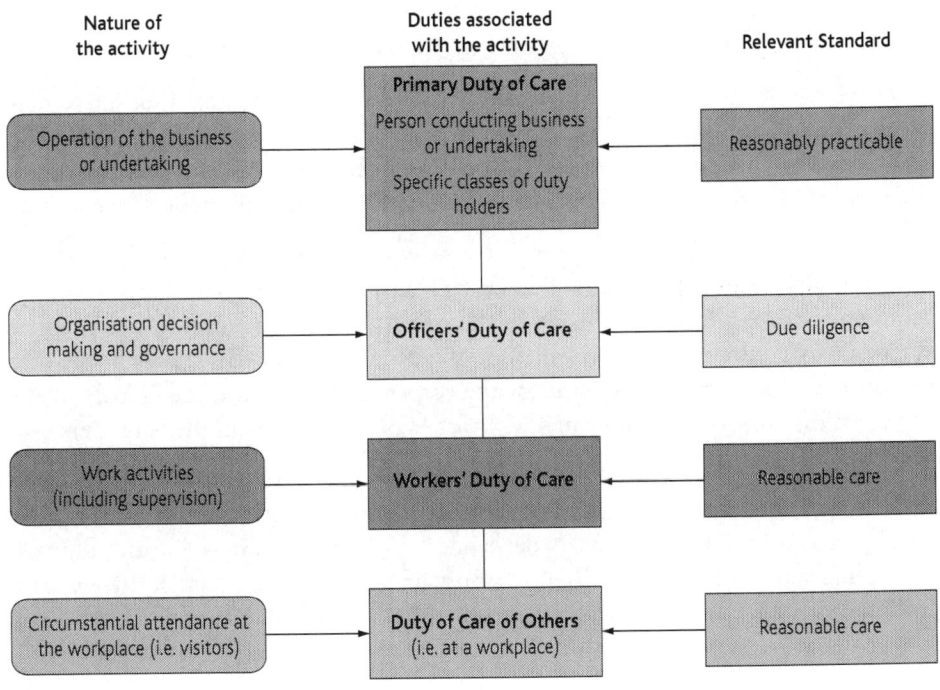

1   Source: Workplace Relations Ministers' Council, *National review into model occupational health and safety laws: second report to the Workplace Relations Ministers' Council* (Second Report), Canberra, WRMC, January 2009, p 68.

This chapter considers the duties of care of those people or entities in whose business or undertaking work is done, or who provide the means by which work is able to be done. These are described as the "primary duty of care"[2] and the "further duties of persons conducting businesses or undertakings" (which are subsets of the primary duty of care).[3]

Rationale for the primary duties of care

Work health and safety laws are directed at the conduct of those who may affect health and safety through their influence over or direction of work and the way in which it is done. The duties of care are related to the role of each of the contributing parties and the things that they are able to direct, control or influence.

The elements of work are:

- where and when the work is done;
- by whom the work is done (including their skills and experience);
- how the work is done (systems of work); and
- with what the work is done (equipment, parts and ingredients).

These elements are the subject matter of the duties of care, as health or safety may be ensured or compromised by decisions made in relation to them. The person or entity who is requiring the work to be done will determine and give directions on each of these elements. That person or entity should, therefore, owe a duty of care.

The primary role of this duty holder will also extend beyond the immediate requirements for the specific work to the organisational and procedural enablers for work to be done. These will include the physical and financial resources that are available for work, the systems for the organisation of work, the culture of the organisation, and the relationships with other parties (for example, suppliers and contractors).

Others who contribute to work being done (for example, a worker who undertakes specific activities), or who make decisions on how a business is run (officers, individually and collectively), also owe a duty of care. However, each of these people undertakes their role as part and for the benefit of the overall business. They will be

---

2 Model WHS Act, s 18.
3 Model WHS Act, s 19–25.

unlikely to have all relevant knowledge or the ability to direct, control or influence all relevant matters. The overarching role of the business operator, along with the associated knowledge of all aspects of the work and control or direction over the elements noted above, justify that person or entity having a broader duty of care.

Current OHS legislation refers to a "general" duty of care. The model WHS Act instead refers to a "primary" duty of care in order to confirm the primacy of this duty above all others (as demonstrated in the diagram at p 15 of this chapter). The use of the expression "general" does not make this clear.

The primary duty of care is applicable not only to the person or entity for whom specific work is done, but also to those who provide the workplace, plant, substances or advice that enable the work to be done. Again, it is at the organisational level, rather than at the individual level, that the matters relevant to health and safety are determined and it is for the organisation that the work is done.

As will be discussed below, those who are subject to the primary duty of care may also be subject to a duty of care relating to their specific activities as a person conducting a business or an undertaking (PCBU), for example, as a designer or manufacturer. As such, they may commit an offence against more than one duty in relation to specific acts or omissions. A prosecutor may accordingly choose to bring a prosecution under one or more provisions of the model WHS Act, but may be more likely to do so for a breach of the primary duty of care as it is broader and the offence may be represented by failings that do not fall within the more specific duty.

The primacy of this duty of care is also evident from its placement in the model WHS Act before all other duties of care.

The rationale for broadening the primary duty beyond that of an employer to employees is to meet the deficiencies of the current general duty noted in chapter 1 — particularly in meeting the changing way in which work is arranged. It is important that the primary duty apply as broadly as possible to ensure the protection of all who undertake or are affected by the undertaking of work.

The qualifier of "reasonably practicable"

The duties of care in the model WHS Act are directed at eliminating or minimising risks to health and safety from the undertaking of work. The fact that a person is exposed to a risk to their health or safety from the undertaking of work does not necessarily mean that a duty holder has been in breach of a duty of care placed on them by the model laws. A breach occurs where the duty holder fails to meet a standard referred to in the specific duty of care.

The primary duties of care are all subject to the qualifier[4] that the duty holder must ensure the relevant matters "so far as is reasonably practicable". Understanding this standard is critical to understanding the reach of these duties of care and what is necessary to comply with them.

"Reasonably practicable" is currently found in all of the principal OHS Acts in Australia and is defined in some of the Acts.[5] The model laws adopt and enhance the existing definitions in the legislation, codifying the interpretation of this qualifier by the courts. The aim of defining the term in this way is to assist the duty holders to understand what they must do.

The definitions of reasonably practicable in the legislation have been consistent with the relevant case law in the United Kingdom and Australia, although they are less extensive (for example, not incorporating the concept of control) and do not provide as much guidance as has been provided by the courts (for example, not referring to the weighing up of relevant considerations).

Section 17 of the model WHS Act describes what is meant by reasonably practicable as follows:

> "In this Act, **reasonably practicable** means that which is, or was, at a particular time reasonably able to be done in relation to ensuring health or safety, taking into account and weighing up all relevant matters including:
>
> (a) the likelihood of the hazard or the risk concerned occurring;
>
> (b) the degree of harm that might result from the hazard or the risk; and
>
> (c) what the person concerned knows, or ought reasonably to know, about:

---

4 As the qualifier of reasonably practicable forms part of the duties of care, the prosecutor in any proceedings for a breach of the duty of care has the onus of proving that the standard has not been met. If the prosecutor fails to satisfy the court that there was something that was reasonably practicable that the duty holder did not do, then the offence cannot be proven. In practice, this is not a heavy burden for the prosecutor to meet. For a discussion of the way in which reasonably practicable qualifies the duties of care and who should have the burden of proof in respect to that element of an offence, see ch 5 of the Workplace Relations Ministers' Council, *National review into model occupational health and safety laws: first report to the Workplace Relations Ministers' Council* (First Report), Canberra, WRMC, October 2008.

5 See, for example, the *Occupational Health and Safety Act 2004* (Vic), s 20(2), and the *Occupational Safety and Health Act 1984* (WA), s 3. Some legislation refers to "practicably" or "taking reasonable precautions", each of which has been interpreted by the courts consistently with the interpretation of "reasonably practicable".

(i) the hazard or the risk; and

(ii) ways of eliminating or minimising the risk; and

(d) the availability and suitability of ways to eliminate or minimise the risk; and

(e) after assessing the extent of the risk and the available ways of eliminating or minimising the risk, the cost associated with available ways of eliminating or minimising the risk, including whether the cost is grossly disproportionate to the risk."

While the relevant matters noted in (a) to (e) are found in current definitions of reasonably practicable, the model laws will provide more explanation of those matters and greater guidance as to what to do when considering those matters. Important elements of section 17 are:

- reference to the particular time at which the assessment is to be made (by referring to "reasonably able to be done") — emphasising that there is a need to look at what is possible and whether or not what is possible ought reasonably be done;

- the need to weigh up all relevant matters (not only those listed);

- that cost is only to be considered after assessing the risk and available risk controls; and

- reference to a consideration of the various available ways of eliminating or minimising the risk.

The definition of reasonably practicable does not include a reference to control. The Panel that undertook the national review into model OHS laws noted case law,[6] indicating that the issue of control is an element of what is reasonably practicable. An absence or limitation of control may be relevant to what a duty holder can do, while a limitation on the control able to be exercised by the duty holder may be relevant to what may *reasonably be able to be done* by them.[7] Note also that the "Principles that apply to health and safety duties" refer to a duty holder being required to discharge the duty "to the extent to which the person has the capacity to influence and control the matter...",[8] thereby recognising that control is a limiting factor in determining what reasonably can be done.

---

6   For example, *R v Associated Octel Limited* [1994] 4 All ER 1051 at p 1063, and *R v ACR Roofing Pty Ltd* [2004] 11 VR 187 at p 214.

7   See the discussion on this issue at pp 45–46 of the First Report.

8   Model WHS Act, s 15(3)(b).

The primary duty of care

Who will owe the duty

Current OHS legislation in Australia provides for the most detailed duties of care to be owed by an employer to its employees (sometimes deemed to include contractors and their employees). Those duties of the employer are accompanied by a broader and less detailed duty owed by the employer (and a self-employed person) to people other than their employees.[9] The duties of care owed by an employer to its employees clearly arise out of the employment relationship and therefore the conduct of a business or an undertaking by the employer. The duties of care owed by an employer to people other than its employees are limited to risks arising from the conduct of the business or undertaking of the employer (chapter 1 identified the concerns that have arisen about the limitations of this approach for the coverage of all who undertake work or are affected by it).

A trend has emerged in recent years to break the reliance on the employment relationship to determine the duty of care owed to people who are undertaking work, or affected by work undertaken, in a business or an undertaking. This has occurred in the legislation in Queensland,[10] the Northern Territory[11] and the Australian Capital Territory.[12] The way in which these provisions have been cast, including the associated definitions, has limited the extent of their coverage.

Section 18 of the model WHS Act reflects the view expressed by the Panel[13] that the employment relationship no longer adequately protects the health and safety of those engaged in or protected by work, and should be replaced by the concept of a "person conducting a business or an undertaking" (PCBU).

The primary duty of care is an amalgamation of the duties owed by an employer to its employees, by an employer to people other than its employees, and of a self-employed person to others. However, the primary duty of care goes further, in that people or entities who are not an employer or a self-employed person but who are conducting a business or an undertaking will also owe the duty of care.[14]

---

9   See, for example, the *Occupational Health and Safety Act 2000* (NSW), s 8(2), the *Occupational Health and Safety Act 2004* (Vic), s 23 and 24, the *Occupational Safety and Health Act 1984* (WA), s 21(2), the *Occupational Health Safety and Welfare Act 1986* (SA), s 22, and the *Occupational Health and Safety Act 1991* (Cth), s 17.

10 *Workplace Health and Safety Act 1995* (Qld), s 28 and 29.

11 *Workplace Health and Safety Act 2007* (NT), s 30, 55–57 and 60.

12 *Work Safety Act 2008* (ACT), s 21.

13 In ch 6 of the First Report.

14 For example, an authority that is regulating certain activities and engaging a contractor to undertake certain elements of those activities, where that authority does not have any employees and may not be considered to be "self-employed".

The primary duty of care will apply to those for whom the work is being done. It will also apply to those who are providing or contributing to (as part of a business or an undertaking) the things that enable work to be done. This will include those who have a role (for example, designers, manufacturers or suppliers) in the availability of things used for or in a process, those who provide the workplace, those who contribute to the process by which work is done (for example, providing advice or systems of work), or those who provide health and safety-specific services (for example, atmospheric monitoring).

Most of those who, in the course of a business or an undertaking, provide or contribute to each of these activities explicitly owe a duty of care (as such) under the model WHS Act.[15] The Workplace Relations Ministers' Council decided that those providing OHS services should not have a specific duty of care, as they are already subject to the primary duty of care.

The "further duties" are not described in the model laws as "primary duties". Each of the relevant activities will be the subject of the primary duty of care, and they are owed by PCBUs as they relate to activities undertaken during the conduct of the business or undertaking of a PCBU. Therefore, they are, in effect, subsets of the primary duty of care.

A PCBU may be guilty of an offence for failing to comply with the primary duty and a specific duty in respect of the same activities and circumstances. This is similar to the current position where an employer may be in breach of its duty to people other than its employees, and in breach of its duty as a designer or supplier, etc, in respect of the same matter. The current practice, whereby the regulator will pursue a prosecution for one or the other breach, or a court will take into account the fact that the breaches arise from the same set of facts when determining the appropriate penalty, should continue.

Who will be a PCBU?

A key part of identifying who a PCBU will be is determining what "a business or an undertaking" is. The model WHS Act does not define this expression, other than to indicate some of the characteristics of a business or an undertaking and when a person or an entity is not conducting one. Recommendation 83 of the Panel provided a definition of a business or an undertaking (consistent with the views expressed by the Panel),[16] but that definition has not been adopted in the model laws.[17]

---

15   Model WHS Act, s 19–25.
16   See the discussion at para 6.54 of the First Report, and pp 53–56 of the Second Report.
17   The definition in the model WHS Act is not inconsistent with that recommended by the Panel, but is briefer and less informative.

The term "business" is well known and it is understood as meaning a commercial, for profit enterprise. The term "undertaking" is intended to imply something broader. The model WHS Act recognises this by providing that a person conducts a business or an undertaking, whether or not it is conducted for profit or gain. The Second Report[18] includes references to these terms in current legislation, dictionary definitions and case law, which we consider will be useful when determining what an undertaking is.

A significant issue (which was raised in written submissions to the Panel and during the drafting of the model laws) is the extent to which, or circumstances in which, a charitable, sporting or social organisation may be a PCBU.

Current OHS laws that refer to an undertaking do so in the context of an employer's duty of care — the question being whether the relevant activity was part of the undertaking of an employer, not whether the employer is conducting an undertaking. The fact that the current laws relate to an employer demonstrates the limitation of the application of the laws to business or commercial activities.

A person or an entity who is currently subject to OHS laws as an employer or a self-employed person will clearly be a PCBU.

A business or an undertaking is usually determined by reference to the activities carried out by the person conducting it. The Panel noted[19] that "[t]he duty provision should make clear (in the section and/or through definitions) that it covers all activities that are undertaken other than those that are clearly undertaken only for private or social reasons". The model WHS Act excludes from the definition of PCBU a "volunteer association", which means:

> "... a group of volunteers working together for one or more community purposes where none of the volunteers, whether alone or jointly with any other volunteers, employs any person to carry out work for the volunteer organisation."[20]

Although there is some doubt that the definition has this affect, it appears that a charitable, social or sporting organisation should not be a PCBU (for the purposes of the model laws) when it is carrying out purely social or charitable activities. To the extent that it is carrying on activities of a commercial nature (such as operating

---

18   Second Report, pp 43–46.
19   In para 6.54 of the First Report.
20   Model WHS Act, s 5(5). This mixes the activities (community purposes) with the status of the volunteers (not being employers). The engagement of people under a contract of services (rather than employment of them) would allow this exclusion to apply. Conversely, a charitable organisation may be a PCBU by employing a single person.

a bar at a club for funding purposes), a charitable, social or sporting organisation should be considered to be a PCBU.

The definition of a PCBU in the model laws does not provide sufficient clarity and may result in unintended outcomes. This is unfortunate, and the drafters are encouraged to amend s 5 of the model WHS Act to provide clearer guidance as to when a charitable, social or sporting organisation may be considered to be a PCBU. Provision for an exemption for an organisation, or specific activities, may be one way of achieving an appropriate balance between the need to ensure safety at work, while not discouraging charitable or social activities.

The exercise of discretion by the regulators when enforcing the model WHS Act (including the taking of proceedings for a breach, and the exercise of the discretion of the courts in any such proceedings) will be important to ensuring that unjust outcomes do not occur.

Proposed guidance material to be developed by the regulators should clarify whether a person is a PCBU.

The definition of a PCBU in s 5 of the model WHS Act makes it clear that this does *not* include a person who is conducting the business or undertaking where they are engaged solely as a worker in, or as an officer of, that business or undertaking. Workers or managers within a business are accordingly not to be considered to be a PCBU. The current position, at least in Victoria, where a "person with management or control of a workplace"[21] can be an individual working within a business, rather than the business itself,[22] cannot occur under the model laws as such a person would not be a PCBU.

A person may be a PCBU (as defined) whether the person conducts the business or undertaking alone or with others. There will often be circumstances where work activities are undertaken as part of a business or an undertaking of a number of parties (for example, a principal, a contractor, a labour provider, and/or the person with management or control of the workplace at which the work is being undertaken). There may accordingly be several PCBUs owing a duty of care to the same people concurrently, and they must each comply with their duty, notwithstanding that other people also have a duty.[23]

To whom will the duty be owed?
Section 18 of the model WHS Act provides that a PCBU must ensure, so far as is reasonably practicable, the health and safety of workers engaged or caused to be

---

21   *Occupational Health and Safety Act 2004* (Vic), s 26.
22   See *R v Guthrie, Stanley and Manumatic Industries Pty Ltd* [2008] VCC 1551.
23   Model WHS Act, s 15.

engaged by them and workers whose activities in carrying out work are influenced or directed by them, while the workers are at work in the business or undertaking.

Workers are defined[24] to mean any person who carries out work in any capacity for a PCBU, and may include not only an employee but also, for example, a contractor, an employee of a labour hire company, an apprentice or a trainee, a student gaining work experience, or a volunteer.[25] That is, a PCBU owes the primary duty of care to any person who is undertaking work as part of, or within the business or undertaking of, that PCBU — however it is that the person comes to be doing so.

Section 18 of the model WHS Act also requires a PCBU to ensure, so far as is reasonably practicable, that the health and safety of other people (that is, other than workers) are not put at risk from work carried out as part of the conduct of the business or undertaking.

Elements of the primary duty of care

The primary duty of care commences by placing broad obligations on a PCBU to ensure, so far as is reasonably practicable:

1. the health and safety of workers engaged or caused to be engaged by the PCBU, and workers whose activities in carrying out work are influenced or directed by the PCBU, while the workers are at work in the business or undertaking;[26] and

2. that the health and safety of other people are not put at risk from work carried out as part of the conduct of the business or undertaking.[27]

The first part of this clearly applies to the PCBU for whom work is being done, while the second part applies to another PCBU whose work affects the work of the PCBU for whom the workers are working (for example, another contractor on a building site) and a PCBU who is subject to one of the "further duties".

Specific elements of the primary duty of care are then set out in s 18(3) of the model WHS Act, that is, those elements ordinarily found in the duty of care owed by an employer to an employee. The specific elements are:

1. the provision and maintenance of a work environment without risks to health or safety (this relates to the circumstances in which work is undertaken, including things such as the organisational structure, rostering, etc, as well as the physical work environment);

2. the provision and maintenance of safe plant and structures;

---

24   Model WHS Act, s 7.
25   This definition and role of a "worker" is dealt with in ch 4 of this book.
26   Model WHS Act, s 18(1).
27   Model WHS Act, s 18(2).

3. the provision and maintenance of safe systems of work;

4. the safe use, handling, storage and transport of plant, structures and substances;

5. the provision of adequate facilities for the welfare of workers when they are carrying out work for the business or undertaking (including access to those facilities);

6. the provision of any information, training, instruction or supervision that is necessary to protect all people from risks to their health and safety arising from work carried out as part of the conduct of the business or undertaking; and

7. the health of workers and the conditions at the workplace are monitored for the purpose of preventing workers from becoming ill or sustaining injuries from the conduct of the business or undertaking.

The primary duty of care requires that each of these elements must be ensured by a PCBU, so far as is reasonably practicable, not only in respect of their workers, but also in respect of people other than their workers.[28] While it may often be unnecessary or onerous for a PCBU to provide training and instruction to a visitor to the workplace, the provision of information through induction may be a critical safety measure at hazardous facilities such as mines, smelters, refineries, etc. Information that is to be provided by way of signage should be clear to visitors and, as they may not be familiar with the relevant operations and risks, the signage may need to be more detailed than if only workers accessed the relevant area. Where workers would be provided with personal protective equipment to minimise risks from chemicals at a workplace, care should be taken to store them in an area that is not accessible to visitors who may not have that protection. It is in these respects that the qualifier of reasonably practicable is particularly significant, given the limitations on the ability of a PCBU to influence or direct the conduct of visitors in some circumstances.

It is important to note that each PCBU must only comply with the primary duty of care by *ensuring*, so far as is reasonably practicable, the health and safety outcomes, the provision of the relevant matters (for example, safe plant and safe systems of work), or that the relevant steps are taken. Where there are multiple duty holders in respect of the same activities, a PCBU may comply with the duty of care by ensuring that the relevant matters are attended to by another person. For example, a PCBU

---

28 Note that the sample clause at para 6.125 of the First Report provided for the duty to be owed to workers "and any other persons", making it clear that the duty is owed to each of these classes. In separating these two elements, the drafters have, in s 18(2) of the model WHS Act, removed the link between workers and "other persons". Arguably, s 18(1) of the model WHS Act may be unnecessary as "other persons" in s 18(2) could be interpreted to mean people other than the PCBU, which would include workers.

may not have to actively take any steps for the provision of safe plant or welfare facilities if another PCBU is doing so. However, the PCBU may be in breach of the duty of care if they do not *ensure* that that occurs, and must therefore take steps to identify and verify the steps that are taken by others to meet the obligation.

The requirement to ensure, rather than necessarily provide, is significant to the provision of welfare facilities. A PCBU may comply with their obligation under (5) above if they ensure that relevant facilities are available, for example, medical services at a nearby clinic or hospital.

The primary duty of care also includes specific obligations for a PCBU to maintain residential premises that are occupied by a worker if the premises are owned by or under the management or control of the PCBU, and if the occupancy by the worker is necessary for the purposes of the worker's engagement with the PCBU because other accommodation is not reasonably available.

Finally, for avoidance of doubt, the primary duty of care requires that a self-employed person must also ensure, so far as is reasonably practicable, their own health and safety while at work.

Elements of the duties related to specific activities of primary duty holders

Arguably, it is unnecessary for the model laws to include the specific duties of care of a PCBU relating to specific activities, as they are subject to the primary duty of care. The model laws do, however, include duties of care for each the following activities of a PCBU:

- the management or control of workplaces, or of fixtures, fittings or plant at workplaces;
- the design, manufacture, importation or supply of plant, substances or structures for use at or as a workplace; and
- the installation, construction, commissioning, decommissioning or dismantling of plant or structures at a workplace.

There are two reasons why the specific duties are included in the model WHS Act, in addition to the primary duty of care:

1. it is important to ensure that those carrying out the relevant activities understand that they do owe the duty of care;[29] and

---

29 For example, designers of buildings or structures intended to be used as a workplace were subject to s 22 or 23 of the *Occupational Health and Safety Act 1985* (Vic). When the specific duty of care was introduced in s 28 of the *Occupational Health and Safety Act 2004* (Vic), relevant industry bodies and individuals complained about the placement of a "new" duty on them.

2. this allows for specific measures to be required of those people as are necessary to eliminate or minimise the risks associated with the particular activity. It would not be appropriate or convenient to include these specific requirements in the primary duty of care, as they would not apply beyond the specific activities.[30]

The specific actions required to be taken by the duty holders are relevant to the nature of the subject matter (plant, substance or structure) and are actions that will assist in ensuring that risks to health or safety are eliminated or minimised, so far as is reasonably practicable.

The requirements for various activities associated with plant, substances and structures are all limited to the use of these items at a workplace for a purpose for which the item was designed, and any reasonably foreseeable activity associated with the use for that purpose. The requirements relate to the physical condition of the subject matter (that it is safe and without risks to health), the steps required to verify that condition (for example, examination and testing), and the provision of information to enable safe use.

How do the duties compare with current OHS laws?

The primary duty of care differs significantly from current OHS laws in the following ways:

- the duty does not rely on the employment relationship — rather, it applies to any PCBU, whether the PCBU is an employer or not. It is therefore broader in coverage, and does not permit gaps from the restrictive employment relationship, even with the extended definitions that include contractors;

- the specific detailed requirements of the current duties of care of an employer to employees are made more explicit, and apply (to the extent that they are relevant) to people other than workers. The specific requirements do not explicitly apply to the duty of care of an employer or self-employed person to non-employees (although they may be necessary to meet the duty);

- the primary duty of care will more readily apply concurrently to multiple duty holders, although a number of employers or self-employed persons may currently owe the broad duty to contractors and non-employees;

- it is now clearer that PCBUs need not undertake compliance activities themselves, so long as they are able to ensure that someone else is taking the necessary steps to achieve the outcomes; and

---

30   For example, requirements to undertake risk assessments, testing and the provision of information. The details of these further duties of PCBUs regarding specific activities are similar to existing duties of care in OHS legislation around Australia, although the provisions are structured differently to the way they are found in some of the legislation.

- the obligations relating to the provision of accommodation for workers will apply in all jurisdictions and more broadly in Western Australia (where the obligation currently exists).

The duties of a PCBU in relation to the specific activities will be different in all of the jurisdictions, as none of the jurisdictions currently provides duties in relation to all of these matters. The model WHS Act makes it clearer that the duties are (where this is noted) applicable to any reasonably foreseeable activities associated with uses of plant, substances and structures for the purposes for which they were designed (but not where they are used other than for those purposes).

Implications of the new duties

The model WHS Act will provide for broader coverage of the primary duty of care and other duties of care of PCBUs, removing many of the current limitations and complexities. It will be clearer that all who (as part of a business or an undertaking conducted by them) require work to be done, or determine how it is done or contribute something to use in it, will owe the primary duty of care. All who are involved in or affected by the undertaking of work will be the subject of the duties of care.

The focus should shift from the question "does this apply to me?" to "what should I do?". Legal labels will be replaced by a "cause and effect" approach to determining duties and rights. The change in approach should encourage PCBUs to take a greater interest in the coordination of their activities with those of other duty holders. This will be further encouraged by the obligation of a PCBU to consult, cooperate and coordinate activities with other duty holders.[31]

Employers should not need to take any further steps in relation to their employees than are currently required, other than in relation to accommodation that is provided by them. While they may already have been required to consider the application of the specific requirements to non-employees (to meet the standard of reasonably practicable), it will now be clear that they must do so.

---

31   Model WHS Act, s 45. See also ch 6 of this book.

CHAPTER 3

OFFICERS' DUTY OF CARE

One of the most important reforms of the model Work Health and Safety Act (model WHS Act) is the introduction of a duty of care on officers of companies and other organisations. The introduction of a position duty is new to the workplace health and safety regulatory framework. Its closest counterpart is the duty which the South Australian legislation places on responsible officers. In all jurisdictions, officers are merely attributed liability for conduct that is committed by their company, rather than being allocated a duty in their own right.

This chapter will explore the duty of care of officers in the context of the private sector. Chapter 5 will explore that duty in the context of the public sector as part of the discussion of that sector's safety obligations.

Rationale for the duty of care of officers

The need for senior management to show leadership with regard to the corporate safety agenda is critical to positive safety outcomes, as it is senior management that establishes the conditions for a safe working environment and culture.

A 2003 study into best practices in safety and health among major corporations undertaken by the Conference Board (an international think tank) found that management practices alone are not sufficient to achieve outstanding safety performance. All workers in a company must be engaged and involved. The study concluded that achieving excellence is about empowering everyone — management, supervisors, employees and contractors alike — to make safety and health truly work.[1] This ultimately comes down to the leadership of senior executives in relation to work health and safety.

The report of the independent review panel (chaired by former United States Secretary of State James Baker) into the BP US refineries (Baker Report) went even further. The Baker Report summarised the issue as follows:

> "In a positive process safety culture, all constituencies of the refinery's workforce — from the plant managers to superintendents to HSSE professionals to hourly employees and contractors — regard process safety as a core value, and all levels of the workforce appreciate that

---

1   Whiting, MA and Bennett, CJ, *Driving toward "0": best practices in corporate safety and health*, Conference Board research report no R-1334-03-RR, Washington, US Department of Labor, Occupational Safety and Health Administration, p 4.

process safety expectations are not considered secondary to production goals, budgetary objectives, or other competing considerations. While site leadership is certainly important in establishing a positive process safety culture, the [Baker] Panel believes that leadership from the top of the company, starting with the Board and going down, is essential. In the Panel's opinion, it is imperative that BP's leadership set the process safety "tone at the top" of the organization and establish appropriate expectations regarding process safety performance. Those expectations must reflect an unwavering commitment to process safety and infuse into BP's workforce the mindset that process accidents are not acceptable. Those expectations must also be translated into measurable goals designed to move BP toward the achievement of excellence in process safety performance."[2]

The requirement of safety leadership as a prerequisite for safety outcomes is precisely what makes a positive officer obligation a fundamental feature of an effective safety legal system. It is therefore not surprising that a positive officer safety duty is now a feature of the model WHS Act.

From a legal perspective, the corporate structure has always presented a regulatory challenge.[3] It is often said that a corporation has no body to kick and no soul to damn. It operates through its officers, employees and agents. Senior management determines the direction which a corporation will take on issues. In that regard, the ability to persuade a corporation to comply with legislative requirements depends heavily on the influence that can be exerted on the individuals who stand behind that corporation.[4] Accordingly, the traditional regulatory model has relied on piercing the corporate veil, that is, officers are held liable for contraventions by their corporation. As such, the liability of officers is an attributed liability which is based on their position within the corporation — even if it is based on a failure on their part to prevent the contravention, as it is in most jurisdictions.[5]

---

2   US Chemical Safety and Hazard Investigation Board, *Report of the BP US refineries independent safety review panel* (Baker Report), Washington, US Chemical Safety and Hazard Investigation Board, January 2007, p 60.

3   For a discussion of the rationale for the personal liability of corporate directors and other officers, see Tooma, M, *Safety, security, health and environment law*, Sydney, Federation Press, 2008, pp 161–162.

4   For a discussion of the rationale for personal liability provisions, see Corporations Market Advisory Committee (CMAC), *Personal liability for corporate fault report*, Sydney, Australian Government Publishing Service (AGPS), 2006, pp 26–27. See also CAMC, *Personal liability discussion paper*, Sydney, AGPS, 2005.

5   In the OHS context (except in NSW, Qld and Tasmania), officers are not deemed liable for the offences of the company but, rather, are liable for failing to take reasonable care to prevent the contravention (Victoria, SA, ACT, NT) or for offences committed with their consent, connivance or wilful neglect (WA).

The rationale behind this relies on the limitations of corporate penalties as a deterrent to corporate wrongdoing. The ability of a company to pass on a penalty through its economic activities (for example, through higher prices to consumers) makes corporate penalties less effective as a deterrent. This is especially the case in monopoly or oligopoly markets. Indeed, if corporate penalties were the only remedy available to secure corporate compliance, the likely penalty may well be factored in as an input cost of production. The imposition of personal liability for corporate offences can act as a more effective deterrent in those circumstances.

The approach taken by the model WHS Act, however, emphasises the corporate governance responsibilities of officers. The personal liability in that context reflects the culpability of company officers in failing to meet their corporate governance responsibilities by preventing the corporate misconduct. Consistent with this rationale, officers under the model laws will have a duty to ensure due diligence. Thus, their attributed liability is transformed into a positive duty to ensure corporate compliance through sound corporate governance.

Chapter

3

In its deliberations on this issue, the Panel that undertook the national review into model OHS laws made the following observations regarding the rationale for a positive safety obligation on officers:

> "The provision creates a positive duty which is seen to apply immediately, rather than accountability only applying after a contravention by the company. The duty would make clear that the officer must be proactive in taking steps to ensure compliance by the company. The standard of 'due diligence' is well known by those who would be sufficiently directing or influencing the decisions of the company as to be defined as 'officers'.
>
> By making the officer liable only for his or her own acts or omissions would provide a sense of control by the officer over their personal liability and a sense of fairness. These elements are each concerns expressed in relation to the 'attributed' liability of an officer.
>
> [The positive duty of officers' option] is more likely than the other options to ensure appropriate, proactive, steps are taken by an officer for compliance by the company with the duties of care placed on the company."[6]

The penalty for breach of such a duty must therefore reflect community expectations that officers will discharge their corporate governance duty. Conversely, the penalty

---

6   Workplace Relations Ministers' Council, *National review into model occupational health and safety laws: first report to the Workplace Relations Ministers' Council* (First Report), Canberra, WRMC, October 2008, p 109.

should reflect community disapproval of officers that fail to do so. Such a penalty should act as both a specific deterrent to the individual to secure greater vigilance on their part in the future, and as a general deterrent to individuals who are in the same position in order to provide them with an incentive to be vigilant in ensuring corporate compliance.[7] This is certainly the case under the model WHS Act, with penalties of up to $600,000 and/or five years' imprisonment being available for breach of the duty of officers.

Duty of officers

Under the model WHS Act, officers of a body must exercise due diligence to ensure that their organisation complies with its duties under the legislation.

Who is an officer?

The duty imposed by s 26 of the model WHS Act is imposed on officers of bodies with duties under the legislation. Bodies include corporations, partnerships and government departments.

The term "officer" has the same definition as it has in the *Corporations Act 2001*, and under this Act, officer means:

- a director or secretary of the corporation;
- a person who makes, or participates in making, decisions that affect the whole, or a substantial part, of the business of the corporation;
- a person who has the capacity to affect significantly the corporation's financial standing;
- a person in accordance with whose instructions or wishes the directors of the corporation are accustomed to act (excluding advice given by the person in the proper performance of functions attaching to the person's professional capacity or their business relationship with the directors or the corporation);
- a receiver, or receiver and manager, of the property of the corporation;
- an administrator of the corporation;
- an administrator of a deed of company arrangement executed by the corporation;
- a liquidator of the corporation; or
- a trustee or other person administering a compromise or arrangement made between the corporation and someone else.

---

7   For a discussion of the limitations of the personal liability regulatory model, see Tooma, op cit, pp 162–172.

The definition is extended to apply to officers of the Crown by s 244 of the model WHS Act. This is discussed further in chapter 5.

What is the duty?

The duty of officers is to exercise due diligence to ensure compliance by their bodies. Due diligence means:

- to acquire and keep up-to-date knowledge of work health and safety matters;
- to gain an understanding of the nature of the operations of the business or undertaking of the body and generally of the hazards and risks associated with those operations;
- to ensure that the body has available for use, and uses, appropriate resources and processes to enable hazards that are associated with the operations of the business or undertaking of the body to be identified and risks associated with those hazards to be eliminated or minimised;
- to ensure that the body has appropriate processes for receiving and considering information regarding incidents, hazards and risks and responding in a timely way to that information;
- to ensure that the body has, and implements, processes for complying with any duty or obligation of the body under this Act; and
- to verify the provision and use of these resources and processes.

These elements are interrelated and cumulative in nature. They are elements of a unified system for ensuring organisational compliance — the essence of due diligence. Each element is discussed further below.

Chapter

3

Acquiring safety knowledge

Due diligence requires officers to acquire and keep up-to-date knowledge of work health and safety matters. This is both in the specific context of their organisation and generally. Ignorance of changes in the law or industry standards is not a defence. Indeed, such ignorance would constitute an offence under s 26 of the WHS Act for failing to exercise due diligence. In a practical sense, this requires officers to engage in a program of training and information monitoring.

Training

Officers need to make themselves aware of changes to legislation and developments in case law, as well as relevant Australian standards. Many organisations address this by regularly briefing their board and executive team, and disseminating publications that provide regular updates on developments in the law and practice in safety.

Safety performance reporting

It is essential that organisations develop reports for monitoring safety performance. Board reports must contain sufficient information in relation to safety performance, including trends in safety performance and emerging issues that require intervention. Executive reports must include more detailed information in relation to safety performance and proactive compliance with safety obligations.

Gaining an understanding of business risks

Due diligence requires officers to gain an understanding of the nature of the operations of the business or undertaking of their organisation, and to develop an understanding of the hazards and risks associated with those operations.

Focusing on major hazards

In practice, focusing on major hazards requires the development of a major hazard plan, that is, a review of the nature of the operations of the business or undertaking and the identification of major hazards associated with the operations. This differs from a risk assessment in that the aim is to identify major hazards which give rise to risks with high consequences, and not necessarily all hazards. Among the latter category, there would be numerous hazards which are associated with low consequences but which have a high-frequency risk profile (a typical example of these are slip and trip hazards). These are over-emphasised in safety management systems and are not the focus of the corporate governance regimes contemplated by the due diligence duty. On the other hand, hazards associated with a high-consequence but low-frequency risk profile are precisely the type of hazards which must be identified by officers in order to satisfy due diligence. Due diligence does not require officers to engage in the routine supervision of work or to interfere with day-to-day management. Rather, it requires officers to introduce the safety checks and balances which are the hallmarks of corporate governance.

Focusing on business operations

The requirement is also commensurate with the business activities. Hazards associated with core business activities must be identified. However, it may be reasonable for matters which are remote to the business to be excluded.

Many business processes, by their very nature, are highly regulated, for example, electroplating, working with molten metal, diving work, high-risk construction work, electrical work, working with hazardous substances, working in confined spaces, and working at heights — to name but a few. Officers must understand the extent to which such processes form part of their business or undertaking and verify that specific legal obligations imposed in relation to such processes are complied with by their organisation.

Providing appropriate resources

Providing appropriate resources that are commensurate with the size and nature of the operation of the business or undertaking is essential to ensuring compliance with the safety duties of officers. It is therefore not surprising that this is core to the definition of due diligence.

Due diligence requires officers to ensure that their organisation has available for use, and uses, appropriate resources and processes to enable hazards that are associated with the operations of the business or undertaking to be identified and managed. At a minimum, this requires recruiting appropriate personnel with relevant safety expertise. In some organisations, it will also mean having such personnel at an appropriate level within the organisation to ensure that safety is taken into consideration during decision-making processes. However, there is more to this element of the duty than simply recruiting personnel. The duty requires adequate and transparent investment in safety infrastructure, processes and systems.[8]

Chapter

3

Resource allocation lessons from the BP Texas City Refinery explosion

No recent case demonstrates the issue of resource allocation more starkly than the circumstances which led to the 2005 explosion at the BP Texas City Refinery in the US. The US Chemical Safety and Hazard Investigation Board's inquiry into the incident found that "cost cutting, failure to invest and production pressures from BP senior executives did not provide adequate resources to prevent major accidents and that budget cuts impaired process safety performance at the Texas City refinery".[9] It is this link with which the resourcing element of due diligence is concerned.

The BP Texas City facility is the third-largest oil refinery in the US. The refinery was originally owned by Amoco and, in 1999, BP acquired the refinery as part of a merger with Amoco. Upon acquiring the Texas City Refinery from Amoco, BP embarked on a program of cost cutting, with a 25% cost reduction in 1999 and further cost cutting initiatives in 2002.[10]

In 2004, BP senior management challenged its North American refineries to cut their capital expenditure estimates for the following year by 25%. Site management at the Texas City Refinery argued against the cuts and managed to secure a concession, with its target being set at 16% rather than the expected 25%.

---

8   See Tooma, op cit, pp 205-208 for a discussion of safety capital.

9   US Chemical Safety and Hazard Investigation Board, *Investigation report: refinery explosion and fire*, Washington, US Chemical Safety and Hazard Investigation Board, March 2007, p 210.

10 For a discussion of the impact of cost cutting on the Texas City Refinery and its link to the incident, see Hopkins, A, *Failure to learn: the BP Texas City Refinery disaster*, Sydney, CCH Australia Limited, 2009, pp 73–83. The following discussion is based on that analysis.

These decisions were made by senior management, which was oblivious to the impact that the cost cuts would have on safety and which also assumed that the cuts would be delivered without compromising safety. But that is precisely what they did.

The cost-cutting initiatives led to waves of staffing cuts, which meant that one operator was charged with monitoring several refinery units as the tragedy unfolded. The cost cuts also led to the learning and development budget being reduced by 50% over the six years preceding the incident. Face-to-face training was replaced with computerised training as part of that cost-reduction strategy — leading to a poor appreciation of the risks associated with the operations. Around the time of the incident, operators would routinely overfill the raffinate splinter tower, believing it to be safer to do this than to insufficiently fill it.

Reductions in capital expenditure meant that the plant was "run to fail" — plant would be kept running until it failed. Only repairs could be justified — not preventative maintenance. Only compliance driven maintenance was undertaken — not design improvements. As such, the blowdown drum was never fitted with a flare (despite this being standard industry practice) because there was no legal requirement to do so. Had that simple change been made, the disaster would have been averted.

It is interesting to note that the Texas City Refinery was a very profitable operation. Indeed, in the year prior to the incident, the refinery had had its most profitable year, generating US$930m to its parent company. This was US$145m more than any other refinery in the BP group. The driver for the cost cutting was not a desire to increase profit per se, but a desire to improve the return on investment. The Texas City Refinery was a large, complex plant, and it therefore had a lot of capital that was tied up. It was also an old plant that required a great deal of capital injection to maintain it. Among the 18 BP refineries worldwide, Texas City was one of the worst performing refineries on a return-on-investment measure because of its size, complexity and age.

On 23 March 2005, senior management's failure to foresee the safety implications of its resource decisions culminated in a disaster that claimed the lives of 15 people and injured 180 others. The explosion was the worst industrial incident in US history.[11] It resulted in a "shelter-in-place" order that required 43,000 people to remain indoors. Houses were damaged as far away as three-quarters of a mile from the refinery. The incident cost BP US$1.5b in financial losses, millions in compensation payments, and US$87m in penalties.

11　The following account comes from the US Chemical Safety and Hazard Investigation Board's inquiry into the incident (*Investigation report: refinery explosion and fire*, Washington, US Chemical Safety and Hazard Investigation Board, March 2007, pp 31-70).

The incident occurred during the start-up of an isomerisation unit after a maintenance outage. Isomerisation is a process used to provide a higher octane component to unleaded gasoline. During the start-up, operators pumped flammable liquid hydrocarbons into the raffinate splitter tower (a vertical distillation column with an inside diameter of 3.8 m and a height of 52 m, and an approximate liquid-full volume of 586,100 L) for over three hours without any liquid being removed — which was contrary to start-up procedure instructions. Critical alarms and control instrumentation provided false indications that failed to alert the operators of the high level in the tower. Consequently, the tower was overfilled and liquid overflowed into the overhead pipe at the top of the tower.

The overhead pipe ran down the side of the tower to pressure relief valves which were located 45 m below. As the pipe filled with liquid, the pressure at the bottom rose rapidly from about 21 pounds per square inch (psi) to about 64 psi. The three pressure relief valves were opened for six minutes, discharging a large quantity of flammable liquid to a blow-down drum which had a vent stack that was open to the atmosphere. The blow-down drum and stack overfilled with flammable liquid, which led to a geyser-like release out of the 34 m tall stack.

Chapter

3

This blow-down system was from the 1950s, and it was antiquated and unsafe in design. It had never been connected to a flare system to safely contain liquids and flammable vapours released from the process.

A pick-up truck, left with its engine idling, provided the ignition source for the flammable cloud which had by then formed around the plant. The resultant explosion and fire engulfed the nearby demountable offices, burning an area of 18,581 m^2.

In a book analysing the incident, Professor Andrew Hopkins made the following observations about BP senior management's approach to resourcing:

> "… senior executives demanded cost cuts and left it to others further down the hierarchy to ensure that these cuts were not at the expense of safety. Lower-level managers responded as best they could to these conflicting requirements but, inevitably, safety was compromised. The only way out of this predicament is for those who order the cost cuts to take responsibility themselves for ensuring that safety is not compromised."[12]

This is precisely what the positive duty of officers seeks to do.

It is important to note that the linking of resourcing with safety duties is not novel. Such a link was made in the context of the duty of care in *O'Sullivan v New South*

---

12   Hopkins, op cit, p 81.

Wales Department of Education and Training,[13] where the NSW Department of Education was prosecuted and convicted for breach of the employer's duty of care for, among other things, failing to provide adequate staffing to ensure the health and safety of employees. The prosecution related to an incident at a special needs school where a teacher's aide who was left alone in charge of a number of physically and intellectually disabled students (some of whom were known to be particularly violent) was attacked by one of the students.

Walton J, VP said, in relation to the failure to provide adequate human resources charge:

> "The real culpability of the defendant, in the context of this charge, relates to Mrs Griffiths' position on 9 February 1999 once Mr McKenzie departed: one of two aides supervising ten students, each of whom was severely disabled, six of whom had severe behavioural disorders, three of whom were known to be violent (albeit that in the case of AK the extent may not have been known), one of whom was known to abscond regularly, and some others of whom were in wheelchairs. That position was simply untenable ... it is clear that the defendant's failure to provide additional human resources to assist Mrs Griffiths in that divided classroom with that complement of students on 9 February 1999 caused the detriment to her safety (the risk) ... The risk ... was patent."[14]

Officers must receive, consider and respond appropriately to information concerning the financial, physical and HR requirements for the effective operation of safety management processes and systems that are relevant to the risks of the business.

Officers are required to ensure that the right people, with the right experience and skills, are in the right places, with adequate resources, to enable health and safety risks to be identified and eliminated or minimised.

As Staunton J observed in *Inspector Mansell v Daly Smith Corporation Pty Ltd*, due diligence is not met by "merely hoping others would or could do what they were told, but also ensuring they have the skills to execute the job they are required to do and then ensuring compliance with that in accordance with the safe standards established".[15]

---

13   *O'Sullivan v New South Wales Department of Education and Training* [2003] NSWIRComm 74.
14   *O'Sullivan v New South Wales Department of Education and Training* [2003] NSWIRComm 74 at [148]–[151]. See *O'Sullivan v New South Wales Department of Education and Training* [2003] NSWIRComm 303 regarding penalty.
15   *Inspector Mansell v Daly Smith Corporation Pty Ltd* [2004] NSWIRComm 349 at [134].

Consideration of incidents, hazards and risks

Due diligence requires officers to ensure that the organisation has appropriate processes for receiving and considering information regarding not only incidents, but also hazards and risks associated with the operations of the business or undertaking of the organisation. That is, there are two aspects to this element of the definition. First, the information on hazards and risks is required in order to constantly monitor hazards and risks as they arise in the business or undertaking. Second, the information on incidents is required to identify deficiencies or failings in existing risk management that need to be addressed.

This element also requires officers to ensure that there are processes for responding in a timely way to that information. This necessarily requires reporting and analysing safety performance.

The Australian standard 1885.1-1990: *Measurement of occupational health and safety performance — describing and reporting occupational injuries and disease*[16] is used as the benchmark for safety performance indicators. It sets out definitions for key measures such as lost-time injury rates,[17] lost-time injury frequency rates,[18] medical treatment injuries,[19] medically treated injury frequency rates,[20] and lost workdays.[21] However, organisations are increasingly aware of the limitations of negative performance indicators as a true measure of safety performance.

The United Kingdom safety regulator, the Health and Safety Executive, summarised the issue as follows:

> "Too many organisations rely heavily on failure data to monitor performance. The consequence of this approach is that improvements or changes are only determined after something has gone wrong. Often the difference between whether a system failure results in a minor or a catastrophic outcome is purely down to chance. Effective management of major hazards requires a proactive approach to risk management, so information to confirm critical systems are operating as intended is essential. Switching the emphasis in favour of leading

---

16 AS 1885.1-1990: *Measurement of occupational health and safety performance — Describing and reporting occupational injuries and disease,* Sydney, Standards Australia, 1990.

17 Occurrences that resulted in time lost from work of one day or shift or more ÷ the number of employees × 100.

18 Lost-time injury rate per million hours worked.

19 Incidents leading to a single injury or multiple injuries requiring treatment by a medical practitioner ÷ number of employees × 100.

20 Number of medically treated injuries in the period per one million hours worked.

21 Number of workdays beyond the day of injury that the employee was away from work because of the injury or illness.

indicators to confirm that risk controls continue to operate is an important step forward in the management of major hazard risks."[22]

The absence of an incident does not necessarily indicate a high level of safety. Indeed, as the Royal Commission into the 1998 Longford disaster[23] observed, management focus on lag indicators such as lost-time injury statistics can hinder the safety agenda, rather than promote it. The explosion at the Longford natural gas plant in Victoria killed two people and injured eight others. The plant had had no lost-time injuries during the previous 12 months, and had received safety awards in recognition of this achievement. Yet a review of its system in the aftermath of the incident revealed serious deficiencies.

Measuring positive performance indicators provides an ongoing assurance that risks are being adequately controlled. It also gives organisations an early warning of any weaknesses in their control systems. This is critical because learning from your mistakes in the context of a major hazard is not a palatable outcome. By giving early warnings of a systems failure prior to the risk crystalising allows organisatons to avoid major incidents.

Officers who focus only on lag indicators therefore cannot have the requisite level of assurance that their company was compliant. In contrast, officers who focus on lead indicators can have a high level of assurance of ongoing compliance.

The difficulty with using positive performance indicators as the sole, or even the main, measure of performance is that these measures are not standardised within or across industries. However, the introduction of the duty of officers (with the implications for the need for systematic monitoring of positive performance indicators) may encourage the development of such standards and the collection of reliable data in this area. In practice, the lack of a standardised approach to lead indicators means that it is necessary and appropriate for officers to monitor both lead and lag indicators as part of exercising due diligence.

Legal compliance

The duty of officers requires them to ensure that the organisation develops, and implements, processes for complying with any legal duty that the organisation has under the model WHS Act. This can only be achieved by undertaking a legal compliance audit of the organisation (that is, a systematic audit of the organisation's policies, procedures and practices using the relevant legal requirement as the standard). For example, in relation to consultation, officers must be satisfied that

---

22   Health and Safety Executive, *Developing process safety indicators*, London, HSE Books, 2006, p 1.
23   Longford Royal Commission, *The Esso Longford disaster gas plant accident: report of the Longford Royal Commission*, Melbourne, Parliament of Victoria, 1999.

procedures and processes have been developed and implemented so that consultation arrangements can be put in place in accordance with the legal requirements under the model WHS Act (discussed in chapter 6). This cannot be done merely by citing a policy, but must be verified in practice across the business or undertaking to ensure, for example, that all people fitting the definition of "worker" are consulted (as required by the model WHS Act). A similar exercise is required in relation to reporting obligations.

Furthermore, once developed, the regulations will prescribe requirements in relation to specified hazards, such as noise, hazardous substances, plant safety, confined spaces, manual handling, electrical safety, major hazard facilities, spray painting, welding, electroplating, molten metal, lead processes, asbestos, abrasive blasting, and construction work. Verification of compliance with these requirements will also be necessary in order to exercise due diligence.

Such audits must be provided and analysed by officers, and any deficiencies closed out.

These audits serve as a verification of compliance by an organisation with its legal obligations. It is not uncommon for an organisation to believe that it is a safe organisation because it has implemented a safety management system based on AS/NZS 4801[24] or a similar standard, but then to discover that it is not compliant with its legal obligations. Ultimately, safety management systems go to one section of the legislation, that is, the primary duty — an important section, but only one section. The balance of the legal obligations, if unchecked, can be missed.

Audit and review

The duty of officers requires more than merely providing systems. It requires verifying the implementation of those systems. Such verification is partly fulfilled through commissioning and monitoring safety audits. But that is not all that the duty requires. The duty requires the personal involvement of officers. Practices such as senior executive participation in "safety observations", for example, are a good way of giving life to that obligation. Ultimately, due diligence is about safety leadership. It is not a duty which can be delegated. It requires officers to take personal responsibility for their organisation's safety performance. Indeed, a recent report into safety practices in the rail industry (arising from a rail crash) goes further in quantifying a minimum requirement for this by prescribing that senior managers should dedicate one hour per week to being personally involved in safety issues with

---

24   AS/NZS 4801-2001: *Occupational health and safety management systems — Specification with guidance for use*, Sydney and Wellington, Standards Australia and Standards New Zealand, 2001.

frontline staff, middle managers one hour per day, and line managers one to two days per week.[25]

How does the new duty differ from the existing laws?

While all Australian jurisdictions impose personal liability on officers in an organisation (except for South Australia), they do not impose a positive duty on officers.[26]

Existing regime

Currently, there are three approaches to the personal liability of officers in the Australian jurisdictions: (1) deemed liability; (2) liability based on failing to take reasonable care to ensure compliance; and (3) liability based on conduct by the officer.

In New South Wales,[27] Queensland[28] and Tasmania,[29] directors and managers are deemed to be liable for OHS offences committed by their company unless they can establish a defence. The defences available are:

- in New South Wales[30] and Queensland,[31] that they were not in a position to influence the conduct of their company in relation to the offence, and in Tasmania,[32] that they had no knowledge of the offence and that it was not reasonable for them to have that knowledge; and

- in New South Wales,[33] Tasmania[34] and Queensland,[35] that they exercised all due diligence.

---

25   Cullen, L, *The Ladbroke Grove Rail Inquiry: part 2*, Norwich, Health and Safety Executive, 2001. For further discussion of management involvement in safety leadership, see Hopkins, op cit, pp 107–120.

26   See also s 53 of the *Workplace Health and Safety Act 1995* (Tas) in relation to responsible officers.

27   *Occupational Health and Safety Act 2000* (NSW), s 26. In NSW, the liability is imposed on directors and people concerned in the management of the corporation.

28   *Workplace Health and Safety Act 1995* (Qld), s 167. In Queensland, the liability is imposed on the executive officers of corporations. However, s 8 and Sch 3 of the Act define an executive officer to mean a person who is concerned with, or takes part in, the corporation's management, whether or not the person is a director or the person's position is given the name executive officer.

29   Section 53 of the *Workplace Health and Safety Act 1995* (Tas) imposes the liability on directors, while s 10–11 create the position of a responsible officer, who is the person with responsibility for the direction and management of the business of the employer at the workplace and on whom an express duty is imposed to ensure compliance by the employer with the duties imposed by the Act.

30   *Occupational Health and Safety Act 2000* (NSW), s 26(1)(a).

31   *Workplace Health and Safety Act 1995* (Qld), s 167(4)(b).

32   *Workplace Health and Safety Act 1995* (Tas), s 53(1)(a).

33   *Occupational Health and Safety Act 2000* (NSW), s 26(1)(b).

34   *Workplace Health and Safety Act 1995* (Tas), s 53(1)(b).

35   Expressed as "reasonable diligence" in Queensland (see *Workplace Health and Safety Act 1995* (Qld), s 167(4)(a)).

In Western Australia,[36] officers will only be personally liable if the offence is committed with their consent or connivance or was due to their neglect.[37]

In Victoria,[38] the Northern Territory, the Australian Capital Territory and South Australia, officers will be personally liable if the contravention is attributable to their failing to take reasonable care.

The only jurisdiction to impose a positive duty on officers is South Australia. In this State,[39] a responsible officer[40] has a duty to take reasonable steps to ensure compliance by their corporation with its OHS duties.

In effect, the duty imposed by s 26 of the model WHS Act adopts the high standard imposed by New South Wales, Queensland and Tasmania, but without adopting the deeming liability approach. That is, the onus of proving due diligence under the model WHS Act will be on the prosecution and not on the defence (as it is in New South Wales, Queensland and Tasmania).

While due diligence has been defined in the model WHS Act, the definition closely mirrors the current definition of due diligence in the case law. In that regard, existing case law on due diligence may serve as a guide to the interpretation of the definition. For example, it is useful to consider the decision of the Land and Environment Court of New South Wales in relation to the meaning and appropriate test for the defence of due diligence under the former New South Wales environmental legislation in *State Pollution Control Commission v RV Kelly*.[41] In that case, Hemmings J held:

> "... due diligence, of course, depends on the circumstances of the case, but contemplates a mind concentrated on the likely risks. The requirements are not satisfied by precautions merely as a general matter in the business of the corporation, unless also designed to prevent contravention. Whether a defendant took the precautions that ought to have been taken must always be a question of fact and, in my opinion, must be decided objectively according to the standard of a reasonable man in the circumstances. It would be no answer for

---

36 *Occupational Safety and Health Act 1984* (WA), s 55. The liability is imposed on any director, manager, secretary or other officer of the body corporate.
37 In the Northern Territory, the liability is limited to wilful neglect.
38 *Occupational Health and Safety Act 2004* (Vic), s 144.
39 *Occupational Health, Safety and Welfare Act 1986* (SA), s 61.
40 A responsible officer is a member of the governing body, a chief executive officer, or a senior executive officer who resides in South Australia, and is appointed as the responsible officer under s 61(1) of the *Occupational Health, Safety and Welfare Act 1986*. If no person in that category resides in South Australia, any officer of the body corporate can be appointed for that purpose. If the corporation fails to make such an appointment, each officer of the body corporate will be deemed to be a responsible officer for the purposes of the Act (see s 61(4)).
41 *State Pollution Control Commission v RV Kelly* (1991) 5 ACSR 607.

such a person to say that he did his best given his particular abilities, resources and circumstances. This particularly applies to activities requiring experience and acquired skill for proper execution."[42]

Is the standard applied by the model WHS Act any less stringent?

The best way to test how the new standard compares with the old is to apply the new test to existing case law. In many respects, the high water mark of the personal liability provisions is reputed to be the New South Wales Industrial Court's decision in *Inspector Kumar v Ritchie*.[43]

It is generally accepted that the New South Wales regime currently imposes the most stringent obligations on directors and people who are concerned in the management of corporations. The application of the new duty to the facts in the Ritchie case[44] gives us a useful reference point as to how far the new duty extends and how it compares with the existing duties. In that case, the managing director of Owens Container Services Australia (Owens) was prosecuted in relation to a breach of the OHS legislation by his company. The case involved an incident in which an employee sustained fatal injuries caused by an explosion at his employer company's Sydney premises.

Owens occupied premises located at the corner of Carnarvon and Newton Streets, Auburn, and conducted a business at that site involving the repair, cleaning and storage of shipping containers and tanks.

The explosion was caused after the employee used a spray gun to spray an amount of methyl ethyl ketone (MEK) into a tank that contained resin solution. Methyl ethyl ketone was regarded as a highly volatile and flammable substance, and had been used as a cleaning agent at the site. The explosion occurred moments after the employee used a high-pressure water spray gun to remove the residual resin.

WorkCover alleged (among other things) that the company and its directors had not provided a safe system of work by reason of a number of failures, including failing to ensure that MEK was not used in confined spaces at a temperature above its flashpoint, failing to ensure that the plant was safe, and failing to ensure the use of safe footwear.

The company pleaded guilty, was convicted and fined $160,000. Its divisional general manager pleaded guilty, was convicted and fined $18,500.

The defendant was a resident of Auckland, New Zealand, and was currently the chief executive officer of a software company unrelated to Owens. He had held this

---

42   *State Pollution Control Commission v RV Kelly* (1991) 5 ACSR 607 at pp 608–609.
43   *Inspector Kumar v Ritchie* [2006] NSWIRComm 323.
44   *Inspector Kumar v Ritchie* [2006] NSWIRComm 323.

position for approximately two years, having become the CEO of the Owens group in October 2001, and ceasing that employment in November 2003 as a result of a takeover of the business.

As CEO, Mr Ritchie dealt with brokers, analysts, major shareholders, banks, customers, suppliers and global partners, as well as the media. The day-to-day operation of the divisions was managed by the general manager of each division relying on people with many years' experience and expertise. As CEO, Mr Ritchie reported to members of the Board, all of whom were non-executive directors.

General managers such as Mr Rose were relied on to inform Mr Ritchie about what was happening in each aspect of the business.

After commencing with the Owens group, Mr Ritchie had investigated OHS in the group, had talked to general managers and others, had considered safety audits, and was informed about what was happening on the ground.

He spent the first two to three months trying to understand the nature of the business and learned about the OHS system, the people running the system, the use of audits, site meetings, and the regulatory provisions.

The HR manager looked at OHS in all divisions. On average, Mr Ritchie met with the HR manager two to three times a week to deal with OHS and other matters.

Monthly reports were received from the heads of each division, and the Executive Committee met each month. The monthly reports and the executive meetings, at Mr Ritchie's initiative, had a specific requirement to deal with OHS issues. Occupational health and safety became a specific agenda item for the Executive Committee.

Occupational health and safety matters were covered in the reports to the Executive Committee and, through this process, Mr Ritchie was able to pick up items from managers and their reports concerning incidents, safety audits, and the safety regulation of the divisions.

There were regular workplace audits to ensure workplace safety and to ensure that the group as a whole was meeting regulatory requirements.

Mr Ritchie set up a cross-functional group to deal with the management of OHS across the business — something that had not been undertaken prior to his appointment as CEO.

Assessments of a number of divisions were made by New Zealand authorities, and some of those divisions had obtained the highest rating in recognition of having achieved best safety practice.

Each month, Mr Ritchie reported directly to the Board, and a report was prepared with the assistance of the company secretary. That report dealt with OHS and relied on reports from the divisions and discussions with divisional general managers.

Mr Ritchie was not, however, personally involved in the OHS of particular businesses because he regarded himself as lacking the specialist knowledge and expertise to undertake that role. That experience, knowledge and expertise was held by the general managers of the divisions, and they had their own specialists who knew the industry and best practice in that industry.

From time to time, Mr Ritchie would also attend the meetings of senior management from each division in order to obtain a view of the particular aspect of the business, to show a willingness to be involved, and to participate in their discussions.

In relation to the overall business of the Owens group, Mr Ritchie said that there were some 80 offices throughout the world. He estimated that he spent between 20% and 30% of his time each year dealing with brokers and analysts, and approximately another 20% to 30% of his time dealing with suppliers, partners and customers.

Mr Ritchie defended the charge on the basis that he was not in a position to influence the conduct of the company in relation to the breach and that he had exercised all due diligence.

He was found guilty and convicted of the charge. Haylen J said:

> "[The defendant]'s position as a Director meant that he had, by virtue of that position, the authority to influence the conduct of the corporation and to do so in relation to this particular contravention. It was within his authority and control to seek to have a policy of safety audits operating at the wash bay sites that addressed the critical issue of earthing and prohibiting the use of MEK or laying down strict procedures for the use of other volatile and dangerous chemicals. [He] was in a position to have reports made to him and policies endorsed addressing each and every aspect of this comprehensive failure by the company. This did not necessarily involve him or require him to become involved in day to day operations in a hands-on way but required effective reporting lines and recommendations from those with expertise in aspects of this specialist operation … As a Director, he had to be active and diligent in requiring information about the nature of that business, the chemicals being addressed, the risks thrown up by having to work with those chemicals, obtaining expert advice as to the best way to remove risks from the operation and ensure the safety of employees at each site. The system should have made him aware of the existence of MEK and how that was to be properly and

safely dealt with when cleaning tanks at any of its sites. He should have been informed of the importance of earthing these facilities and the risks that flowed from not having an effective system of earthing. He should have been informed of the details of appropriate protective work clothing required for this task and the means by which the wearing of this clothing was to be ensured at each site."[45]

In relation to the due diligence defence, his Honour went on to say:

"If the hallmark of this defence is that the defendant would need to show that he had laid down a proper system to provide against contravention of the Act and had provided adequate supervision to ensure that the system was properly carried out, then Mr Ritchie's defence case fails. The evidence does not disclose a director's mind concentrated on the risks of this operation or addressing systems so that those risks will be exposed to the directors in order that they might take steps to address those risks. It cannot be said in the present case that the contravention was due to simple human error of an otherwise particularly well-equipped worker who, had he abided by the system laid down, would have avoided the risks inherent in the operation."[46]

Mr Ritchie was convicted and fined $22,500. But how would he have fared under the model WHS Act?

Applying the new due diligence test, it is not clear that the Ritchie case would have been decided differently. Mr Ritchie had not gained an understanding of the nature of the hazards and risks associated with the operations of the business. In particular, he had failed to understand the hazards associated with the cleaning of containers — a core business for Owens. He had failed to ensure that the company had implemented processes for complying with its legal obligations. In particular, he had failed to ensure that the company had in place processes for undertaking risk assessments in relation to the use of hazardous substances such as MEK — an express legal obligations under the OHS regulations. Finally, while he appears to have reviewed some audit reports, his evidence was that he had left the divisions to the care of the general managers, as he did not feel sufficiently qualified to do so.

As such, even the Ritchie case (the high point of the due diligence definition in New South Wales) may well have been decided in the same way under the model WHS Act. It is not enough for officers to point to general initiatives as constituting compliance with their duty. The duty is onerous and requires vigilance by officers to personally ensure that their organisation is complying with its obligations.

Chapter

3

---

45   *Inspector Kumar v Ritchie* [2006] NSWIRComm 323 at [173].
46   *Inspector Kumar v Ritchie* [2006] NSWIRComm 323 at [177].

CHAPTER 4

RIGHTS AND DUTIES OF WORKERS AND OTHER PEOPLE AT WORKPLACES

The model Work Health and Safety Act (model WHS Act) establishes a regime of responsibilities and obligations which is commensurate with their ability to influence safety outcomes. It also establishes protections for people that are aimed at fostering an environment where safety issues can be raised and disputes resolved.

Nowhere is this balance more prevalent than in relation to the rights and obligations of workers. Onerous as it is, the regime created through the duty of a person who is conducting a business or an undertaking (PCBU) would be incomplete without placing obligations on workers with respect to their own conduct, and providing protections to workers to create an environment where safety issues can be brought to the attention of PCBUs. This chapter discusses that combination.

Why impose a duty on workers and other people at workplaces?

Workers are at the coalface of the business or undertaking conducted by a PCBU. In that respect, even the best system cannot be completely effective without the cooperation and engagement of the workers themselves. Indeed, worker behaviour is a prerequisite to safety culture in any organisation. The engagement of workers ensures effective implementation of the policies and procedures that form part of the safety management system. To paraphrase Professor James Reason, the attitude and alertness of workers to risks can continue to propel the system towards the goal of maximum safety, regardless of the organisation's leadership or the current commercial concerns.[1] The proactive involvement of workers in identifying and addressing safety risks greatly assists the PCBU in managing safety at the workplace.

The conduct of workers also has an impact on the health and safety of others at the workplace. Any legal duty which helps to focus workers' minds and aligns their moral and corporate responsibilities with their legal responsibilities is therefore welcomed. This is the essence of the duty of workers under the model WHS Act, and it is the reason why this issue had a high degree of unanimity in public submissions made

---

1   Reason, J, *Managing the risks of organizational accidents*, Williston, VT, Ashgate Publishing Company, 1997, p 195.

to the Panel that undertook the national review into model OHS laws. As the Panel noted in its First Report:

> "The majority of submissions to the review, across all stakeholder groups, indicate support for inclusion of a duty for workers to take reasonable care for the health and safety of others at the workplace. Of these, most thought that workers should also be required to take reasonable care of themselves."[2]

Accordingly, the Panel recommended that:

> "The model Act should place on all persons carrying out work activities ("workers") a duty of care to themselves and any other person whose health or safety may be affected by the conduct or omissions of the worker at work."[3]

Section 27 of the model WHS Act gives effect to that duty.

The Panel also considered whether other people at the workplace should have a duty under the model laws. The Panel observed that:

> "Submissions were divided on whether the model Act should contain a duty of care for 'others' at a workplace (those who are not workers and would not otherwise be a duty holder under the model Act e.g. visitors to a workplace). Those who favour the inclusion of a duty for 'others' propose that such persons should be required to take care for their own health and safety (some suggesting this be that they are not reckless), and be required to follow instructions related to health and safety. Those opposed to placing a duty of care under the model Act on 'others' argue that the duty would be unnecessary as it is provided for at common law."[4]

The Panel preferred the former view and recommended the inclusion of a duty on people at the workplace. The Panel commented:

> "We consider the duty owed by other persons should be similar to that of a worker, but without the requirement to report unsafe conditions, etc.

2   Workplace Relations Ministers' Council, *National review into model occupational health and safety laws: first report to the Workplace Relations Ministers' Council* (First Report), Canberra, WRMC, October 2008, p 114.
3   First Report, p 116.
4   First Report, p 114.

The reasons for requiring other persons to take reasonable care for themselves and other persons at work are similar to those relating to the duty of care of a worker. Similarly, a failure by an 'other person' at a workplace to cooperate with any reasonable action taken by the person conducting the undertaking (or the relevant person) in complying with the model Act may place persons at risk.

Appreciating such persons in this category might include visitors to a worksite or, alternatively, the public (passing by a worksite) who may be affected by the conduct of the undertaking, there are a range of persons that might be captured by this provision. Therefore such a duty of care would be proportionate to any control such a person is able to exercise, recognising that such duties are complementary to the overall duty of the person conducting the undertaking."[5]

The Panel recommended that:

"The model Act should place a limited duty of care on other persons present at a workplace (not being a worker or other duty holder under the model Act) involved in work activity:

(a) to take reasonable care for their own health and safety; and

(b) to take reasonable care that their acts and omissions do not adversely affect the health and safety of others; and

(c) to cooperate with any reasonable action taken by the person conducting the business or undertaking in complying with the model Act."[6]

Section 28 gives effect to that recommendation.

Should workers have the same liability as a PCBU?

Despite the important role that workers play, it is appropriate that the duty and liability of workers should be less than that of a PCBU because their ability to influence safety outcomes is more limited. It is the PCBU who sets the systems, provides the plant, selects the working environment, and determines the conditions in which the workers will work.

The same is also true of visitors at workplaces. They can affect the health or safety of themselves and others from the way they behave. Being new to the workplace, visitors are unfamiliar with the controls that are in place to address the safety risks

Chapter

4

---

5   First Report, p 118.
6   First Report, p 118, recommendation 48.

that may arise from the business or undertaking. Importantly, they are not familiar with the workplace itself. This exposes visitors to more risks than workers at the workplace. It stands to reason, therefore, that visitors should be held to a similar standard as workers, that is, they should be required to follow instructions and take reasonable care for their own safety and the safety of others at the workplace.

Although visitors may not be aware of the policies and procedures at a workplace, they should at least be required to comply with instructions (which may be provided directly to them or through signs at the workplace).

What is the duty of care of workers?

Workers are required to take reasonable care of their own health and safety at work, and to take reasonable care that their own acts and omissions do not adversely affect the health and safety of other people at work. Workers are also required to follow any reasonable instruction to comply with the model WHS Act, or any reasonable policy or procedure relating to work health or safety, that has been given to them by the PCBU.

The duty is therefore the embodiment of the common law duty of care of employees extended to apply to all workers and transformed into a statutory duty imposing criminal obligations. The test for reasonable care is an objective test, that is, the courts will look at what a reasonable person would have done in the circumstances of the worker, rather than looking at the subjective situation of the worker.

Who is a worker?

A person is a "worker" if they carry out work in any capacity for a PCBU. This is an extremely broad definition. It includes work as an employee, a contractor, a subcontractor, an employee of a contractor or subcontractor, an employee of a labour hire company, an outworker, an apprentice, a trainee, a student gaining work experience, or even a volunteer.

The term "work" is not defined. It should therefore be given its ordinary meaning. However, given that the definition of a PCBU is not limited to undertakings for profit, it would follow that the work need not be for gain and reward. Indeed, the definition expressly includes volunteers.

Who is a person at a workplace?

The duty of care of a person at a workplace is intended to capture visitors to workplaces, such as customers and clients, passers-by, relatives and associates of workers, and trespassers. Unlike the term worker, the phrase "person at a workplace" is not defined. However, the duty is imposed on a person and, by its construction, is intended to apply to natural people. The lynchpin of the duty is the definition of "workplace". Since the duty applies only where a person is at a workplace, its scope depends entirely on the definition of workplace. This is discussed below.

What is a workplace?

A workplace is defined as a place where work is carried out for a business or an undertaking. It includes any place where a worker goes, or is likely to be, while at work (for example, a vehicle, a vessel, an aircraft or other mobile structure, any waters and any installation on land, and on the bed of any waters or floating on any waters). As such, not only are factories, shops, construction sites and offices workplaces, but roads, homes, national parks, schools, hotels, airports, aeroplanes, ports and ships are also workplaces when people are working there. Indeed, any place can be transformed into a workplace if people work there.

This broad interpretation has significant implications to the duty of people at workplaces. This is discussed below.

Chapter

4

What is the duty of people at workplaces?

A person at a workplace has a similar duty to that of a worker. They are required to take reasonable care with respect to their own health and safety, and to take reasonable care not to adversely affect the health and safety of other people at the workplace. They are also required to follow the reasonable directions of the PCBU.

How do the duties compare with existing duties?

The duty of workers mirrors the current duty of employees in most Australian jurisdictions and, in that respect, it does not represent a significant change. The difference between the model laws and the current regime is the definition of worker. That definition brings anyone who performs work (including those who do so as volunteers) within the scope of the duty. Many would be caught by other duties, such as the duty currently imposed on self-employed people. Others, such as employees of a contractor, subcontractor or labour hire company, already fall within the scope of the existing duty of employees.

Duty of volunteers

Volunteers have largely fallen outside the duties imposed by the current OHS legislation. As such, the inclusion of volunteers in the model WHS Act represents a significant change in their liability. For example, volunteer firefighters may be liable for a criminal offence if they fail to take reasonable care with respect to the health and safety of a person during a bushfire. Equally, volunteer lifesavers may be criminally liable if they fail to take reasonable care with respect to the health and safety of a swimmer during a rescue, if they are considered to be carrying out "work".

Contractors will have a right to cease work

Of greater interest is the ability of workers to exercise the right to cease work on safety grounds and to enjoy the full extent of the protections afforded on the exercise of this right (including protection against discrimination). To date in most Australian jurisdictions, this has been the right only of employees. The extension of the definition of worker, however, affords that right to contractors and subcontractors.

Duty of home occupants

Importantly, expanding the category of duty holders to include people at the workplace has the potential to capture classes of people and activities which have, until now, remained outside the reach of the OHS legislation. Consider, for example, the activities of a tradesperson at a home. The tradesperson is a PCBU. They and/or their employees are workers under the model WHS Act. Their work activities at the home therefore render the home a workplace. As such, residents at the home are people at a workplace, and they are therefore subject to the duty to take reasonable care of their own health and safety, and to take reasonable care not to adversely affect the health and safety of others. Notably, they are required to follow the reasonable directions of the PCBU in relation to safety matters.

The same analysis is true of housekeepers, gardeners, home-carers and babysitters, as well as home-based businesses and people working from home. In that respect, the duty of people at a workplace captures classes of people who had previously been outside the reach of OHS laws.

It is important to note that these people will each be required to meet the standard of reasonable care, which will be determined by reference to what a reasonable person in their position would be expected to know. The duty should, therefore, not be unduly onerous and no more so than their duty at common law.

Customers at shopping centres are duty holders

There is little doubt that a shopping centre is a place where workers work. Shopkeepers, cleaners, facilities managers, maintenance staff, marketing personnel, and centre management staff are all workers working at the shopping centre for various PCBUs. In that context, a customer is a person at a workplace and, as such, they have a duty under the model WHS Act to take reasonable care with respect to their own health and safety and the health and safety of others. They also have a duty to follow the reasonable instructions of PCBUs in relation to safety matters. Like any other breach of the model laws, failure to do so is a criminal offence.

Union activities may be caught

The introduction of the duty of people at a workplace not only captures clients and visitors at the workplace, but it also captures union officials. Indeed, the duty may be relevant to and part of the approach of some PCBUs in managing industrial matters and, in particular, their dealings with unions. That potential flows from the duty to take reasonable care not to adversely affect the health and safety of other people at the workplace.

In saying this, we are not suggesting that union officials would deliberately misconduct themselves and put others at risk, or that PCBUs would seek to manipulate circumstances or inappropriately seek to use the model laws for purposes that are not health or safety related. It is simply important to understand that the proper application of the model laws may impact on other aspects of the relationships of those in the workplace, and activities that they may otherwise be engaged in.

Chapter

4

Consider the application of the duty in the context of a picket line. The definition of a workplace is broad enough to capture surrounding areas, including access and egress to the workplace. The very existence of a picket line may have the potential to adversely impact the health and safety of people at the workplace — let alone any obstruction of access typically associated with picket lines. The reach of OHS laws in this context had previously been limited because the duties which existed applied to workers and, often, workers themselves do not staff such picket lines. The introduction of the duty of other people may, therefore, offer an interesting application of the model laws to an age-old industrial challenge.[7]

Right to cease work

In addition to the duties imposed on them, workers are afforded the right to refuse or cease unsafe work.[8] If a worker has reasonable concern that to carry out certain work would expose the worker to a serious risk to their health or safety (emanating from an immediate or imminent exposure to a hazard), the worker may cease or refuse to do the work. In those circumstances, the worker must, as soon as possible,

---

7   It is arguable that union officials, as employees of unions, would owe a duty of care under existing laws.

8   The right to cease work is discussed further in ch 6.

notify the PCBU that they have ceased work for safety reasons, and they must remain available to carry out suitable alternative work as directed. The worker's continuity of engagement will not be impacted by that decision.

The PCBU is not precluded from allocating alternative work to a worker who has ceased work on safety grounds, provided the alternative work is safe and appropriate for the worker to carry out. The work may be at the same workplace or at another workplace.

As discussed in chapter 6, a health and safety representative may direct a worker (who is in a work group represented by the representative) to cease work if the representative has a reasonable concern that to carry out the work would expose the worker to a serious risk to the worker's health or safety (emanating from an immediate or imminent exposure to a hazard). However, the health and safety representative must not give the worker a direction to cease work unless the matter is not resolved after consulting about the matter with the PCBU for whom the worker is carrying out the work, and after attempting to resolve the issue using the issues resolution framework prescribed under the model WHS Act.

The health and safety representative may direct the worker to cease work without carrying out that consultation or attempting to resolve the issue if the risk is so serious and immediate or imminent that it is not reasonable to consult before giving the direction. If that is the case, the health and safety representative must carry out the consultation as soon as possible after giving that direction.[9]

The worker, health and safety representative or the PCBU may ask the regulator to appoint an inspector to attend the workplace to assist in resolving an issue arising in relation to the cessation of work.

Protection against victimisation

In order for an organisation to have a safety culture, it must promote an informed culture,[10] a reporting culture,[11] a learning culture,[12] a just culture,[13] and a flexible

---

9   Note the training requirements in relation to health and safety representatives.

10   An informed culture involves creating a safety information system that collects, analyses and disseminates information from incidents and near misses, as well as from regular proactive checks on the system's vital signs.

11   A reporting culture requires a climate where people are prepared to report their errors and near misses.

12   A learning culture requires an organisation to be able and willing to draw the right conclusions from its safety information and to implement corresponding reforms.

13   A just culture depends on an atmosphere of trust in which people are encouraged to provide safety-related information and where there is a clear line between acceptable and unacceptable behaviour.

culture.[14] This can only happen if workers feel that they are able to raise safety concerns without fear of recrimination.

In its inquiry into the safety culture at BP's United States refineries in the aftermath of the Texas City Refinery explosion (the Baker Report), the independent review panel observed that:

> "[A] good safety culture requires a positive, trusting, and open environment with effective lines of communication between management and the workforce, including employee representatives. The single most important factor in creating a good process safety culture is trust. Employees and contractors must trust that they can report incidents, near misses and other concerns — even when it reflects poorly on their own knowledge, skills, or conduct — without fear of punishment or repercussion. The workforce must trust that when provided with such information, management will investigate and use it in order to improve safety and not to assign blame. Management must trust that the workforce is accurately and thoroughly reporting such matters in order to improve safety and learn from mistakes, not simply to obtain some financial or other benefit. Management and labor must trust each other so that safety issues do not become bargaining chips in the pursuit of other goals, and management and employees representatives must communicate well. In additional, management and labor must trust contractors, and vice versa, so that information and lessons learned are properly shared among all workers ..."[15]

The legal basis for that framework is enshrined in the model WHS Act through the victimisation provisions. A PCBU is simply prohibited from discriminating against workers who raise safety concerns — thus providing workers with legally enforceable commitments to foster the trust to which the Baker Report refers. These were the issues which motivated the Panel that undertook the national review into model OHS laws. The following observations were made by the Panel with regard to the rationale for victimisation provisions:

> "We consider, however, that the model Act should include provisions dealing with discrimination, victimisation and coercion related to OHS, because:

---

14 A flexible culture involves an organisation reconfiguring itself in the face of danger, for example, where control passes to task experts on the spot if the circumstances require it.

15 US Chemical Safety and Hazard Investigation Board, *Report of the BP US refineries independent safety review panel* (Baker Report), Washington, US Chemical Safety and Hazard Investigation Board, January 2007, p 75.

Chapter

4

- to do so will directly support involvement in OHS activities and roles, by making clear in the model Act, rather than having to look elsewhere, that the proscribed conduct is unlawful and clearly subject to penalties and remedies;
- there are significant gaps in the availability of remedies under the discrimination laws[16] and the Fair Work Bill;
- other legislation does not provide for the proscribed conduct to be an offence;
- the model Act can provide clarity and detail that is not present in the other legislation, particularly as to the types of conduct that are prohibited and the roles and activities to which the proscribed conduct relates; and
- the model Act can provide an alternative means of obtaining redress."[17]

Under the model WHS Act, a PCBU must not discriminate against a worker for raising a safety concern. Discrimination is defined broadly to not only include dismissing or terminating the engagement of a worker, but also includes putting a worker in a position that is to their detriment in their engagement, and altering the position of the worker to their detriment. The definition also captures refusing to engage a prospective worker (or treating them less favourably than other prospective workers), or terminating or refusing to enter into a commercial arrangement with a worker. Indeed, a person engages in discriminatory conduct if they organise to take any of these actions, or threaten to organise or to take any of these actions.

An offence is committed if the discrimination arises for any of the following prohibited reasons:

- the person is, has been or proposes to be a health and safety representative or a member of a health and safety committee;
- the person undertakes, has undertaken or proposes to undertake another role under the model WHS Act;
- the person exercises a power or performs a function, has exercised a power or performed a function, or proposes to exercise a power or perform a function as a health and safety representative or as a member of a health and safety committee;

---

16 These will apply to OHS activities only occasionally.

17 Workplace Relations Ministers' Council, *National review into model occupational health and safety laws: second report to the Workplace Relations Ministers' Council* (Second Report), Canberra, WRMC, January 2009, pp 193-194.

- the person exercises, has exercised or proposes to exercise a power under the model WHS Act, or exercises, has exercised or proposes to exercise a power under the model WHS Act in a particular way;

- the person performs, has performed or proposes to perform a function under the model WHS Act, or performs, has performed or proposes to perform a function under the model WHS Act in a particular way;

- the person refrains from, has refrained from or proposes to refrain from exercising a power or performing a function under the model WHS Act, or refrains from, has refrained from or proposes to refrain from exercising a power or performing a function under the model WHS Act in a particular way;

- the person assists, has assisted or proposes to assist, or gives, has given or proposes to give any information to, any person exercising a power or performing a function under the model WHS Act;

- the person raises, has raised or proposes to raise an issue or a concern about work health or safety with a PCBU, an inspector, a work health and safety entry permit holder, a health and safety representative, a member of a health and safety committee, another worker, or any other person who has a duty under the model WHS Act in relation to the matter or any other person exercising a power or performing a function under the model WHS Act;

- the person is involved in, has been involved in or proposes to be involved in resolving a work health or safety issue under the model WHS Act; or

- the person is taking action, has taken action or proposes to take action to seek compliance by any person with any duty or obligation under the model WHS Act.

It is also an offence to request, instruct, induce, encourage, authorise or assist another person to engage in such discriminatory conduct.[18] As is often the case with victimisation provisions of this kind, the onus of proof of the reason for the discriminatory conduct is reversed.[19]

Chapter

4

---

18 See also the prohibition against the coercion or inducement of a person in the exercise of their powers under the model WHS Act (s 107).
19 Model WHS Act, s 109.

CHAPTER 5

PUBLIC SECTOR OBLIGATIONS

The model Work Health and Safety Act (model WHS Act) applies not only to the private sector, but also to the public sector. This has also been the case with the existing OHS laws. The importance of the reforms brought about by the model laws is the application of the personal liability provisions to the Federal public sector for the first time. The model laws also provide clarity as to who within the public sector will be considered to be an officer, and this is explored further in this chapter.

The application of the broad provisions introduced by the model WHS Act to the public sector expands the reach of the public sector's duties, especially the Federal public sector, in significant respects. Whereas, previously, the focus of public sector liability was on its duty as an employer to public sector employees, the introduction of the concept of a person conducting a business or an undertaking as the basis for liability means that every activity of the public sector is caught, that is, both policy activities as well as operational activities.

Indeed, a decision by a government department under a government scheme may have implications for people who are far removed from the department office, but who are nevertheless affected in a direct way by the business or undertaking. These expanded obligations, overlaid with the officers' duties, make the model WHS Act an area of priority for the public sector generally and the Federal public sector in particular.

The model WHS Act binds the Crown

At common law, there is a strong presumption that the Crown is not bound by legislation in the absence of some clear expression of legislative intent or a necessary implication that it should be.[1] Furthermore, there is a strong presumption against attaching a meaning to a statutory provision which would amount to an attempt to impose on the Crown a liability of a criminal nature.[2] Section 9 of the model WHS Act puts both these issues beyond doubt. The section expressly binds the Crown in right of the jurisdiction which is enacting the legislation and the Crown in all its

---

1   *Province of Bombay v Municipal Corp of Bombay* [1947] AC 58; *Bropho v Western Australia* (1990) 171 CLR 1.
2   *Cain v Doyle* (1946) 72 CLR 409 per Dixon J at p 424 (with whom Rich J concurred).

other capacities (in so far as the legislative power of the Parliament permits).[3] The section goes further to make it clear that the Crown is liable for an offence against the model WHS Act.[4] Section 246 of the model WHS Act allows infringement notices to be issued on the Crown.

Section 243 of the model WHS Act goes further by making it clear that, if the Crown is guilty of an offence, the relevant penalty to be imposed on the Crown is that which is applicable to a body corporate. Furthermore, any conduct engaged in or on behalf of the Crown by an employee, agent or officer of the Crown acting within the actual or apparent scope of their authority is deemed by s 243(2) of the Act to be conduct engaged in by the Crown.

A public or local authority is liable to pay any penalty imposed on the authority for an offence against the model WHS Act, and the authority may be issued with an infringement notice.[5]

Under s 245 of the model WHS Act, the agency whose act or omission constituted the offence may be named in proceedings or on notices. Section 245(2) provides for succession for agencies who cease to exist.

The responsible agency in respect of an offence is entitled to act in proceedings against the Crown for the offence and, subject to any relevant rules of court, the procedural rights and obligations of the Crown as the accused in the proceedings are conferred or imposed on the responsible agency.[6] Section 245(4) of the model WHS Act permits the responsible agency to be changed during proceedings with the court's leave.

What is the Crown?

A body can be considered as an emanation of the Crown if it is a branch of a government department (that is, a mere agent of the government) or if it performs inalienable governmental functions.[7] However, a body does not represent the Crown if it is an independent body that is capable of exercising its own discretion, whether or not it is a for-profit body, performs some public function or pays its revenue into the public purse.[8]

---

3   Model WHS Act, s 9(1). As a general rule, a State parliament does not have the power to enact legislation which is binding on the Commonwealth, which defines or regulates the Commonwealth's rights or duties towards its subjects, or which controls or regulates the Commonwealth's governmental rights. See *Commonwealth v Cigamatic Pty Ltd* (1962) 108 CLR 372.

4   Model WHS Act, s 9(2).

5   Model WHS Act, s 247.

6   Model WHS Act, s 245(3).

7   *Skinner v Commissioner of Railways* (1937) 37 SR (NSW) 261.

8   *Skinner v Commissioner of Railways* (1937) 37 SR (NSW) 261 per Jordan CJ at p 270.

The kind of relationship which suffices to confer a Crown attribute on a body in a particular case will vary, depending on the type of attribute claimed.[9] Where a body has several functions, it may be that only some of those functions have attributes of the Crown or, conversely, it may be that only some Crown attributes attach to the body. This is of particular relevance to State-owned corporations, where the degree of ministerial involvement varies from corporation to corporation.

Privilege against self-incrimination

As discussed in chapter 7, under s 171 of the model WHS Act, the privilege against self-incrimination is abrogated, but with a protection that prevents the use of self-incriminating information provided as part of an investigation. However, that privilege, where it is existed at common law, applied only to individuals. Corporations do not enjoy that privilege. So, does the Crown?

As a corporation sole, the Crown does not have a privilege against self-incrimination. Officers and employees of the Crown have the privilege and, under s 171 of the model WHS Act, they enjoy the protection afforded by that section in relation to the use of information provided by them against them — but the Crown does not.[10]

Proceedings against successors to public authorities

The model WHS Act creates criminal offences. Just as criminal liability is extinguished on the death of a natural person, criminal liability is extinguished on the winding up of a company. The same analysis would ordinarily be true for the public sector, that is, criminal liability would be extinguished by the dissolution of a statutory corporation. However, s 248 of the model WHS Act displaces that application.

Under s 248 of the model WHS Act, proceedings for an offence against the Act that were instituted against a public authority before its dissolution, or that could have been instituted against a public authority if not for its dissolution, may be continued or instituted against its successor if the successor is a public authority. Similarly, an infringement noticed served on a public authority for an offence is taken to be an infringement notice served on its successor if the successor is a public authority.[11]

Chapter

5

---

9   *Superannuation Fund Investment Trust v Commissioner of Stamps (SA)* (1979) 145 CLR 330. In *Roads Corporation v Morris Gerkens* (unreported, Supreme Court of Victoria, 28 May 1993), Eames J held that the Roads Corporation was not a manifestation of the Crown in relation to its role of erecting traffic signals.
10 *WorkCover Authority (NSW) v Police Service (NSW)* [2000] NSWIRComm 234.
11 Model WHS Act, s 248(2).

Liability of public sector officers

Who will be an officer?

As discussed in chapter 3, a positive duty is imposed on officers by s 26 of the model WHS Act. The duty requires officers to exercise due diligence to ensure compliance by their company or organisation. Officers are defined by reference to s 9 of the *Corporations Act 2001*. Clearly, that definition, being concerned as it is with officers of corporations or associations, does not cover officers in the public sector and, in particular, officers of the Crown. Section 244 of the model WHS Act addresses this deficiency.

Section 244 provides that a person who makes, or participates in making, decisions that affect the whole, or a substantial part, of the business or undertaking of a government department, public authority or local authority is taken to be an officer of the Crown or that authority for the purposes of the model WHS Act.[12] This definition is remarkably broad in that it merely requires the person to be a person who participates in the making of decisions that affect a substantial part of a government department, public authority or local authority. That will capture all levels of management in a government department, including director generals, secretaries and many executive positions. Within public authorities, many senior managers will also be caught by that definition. It will have the same application to local authorities.

Who will be an officer of a government department or agency will depend on the decision-making structure and processes for the organisation. The Workplace Relations Ministers' Council decided that Ministers of the Crown and local government councillors, who would otherwise fall within the definition of an officer, should not do so. The model laws specifically provide for this in s 244. However, it should be noted that this does not exclude a Minister or councillor from liability as a worker if they are involved in undertaking work (for example, if they involve themselves in the day-to-day activities of the department or council) or as an "other person" at a workplace.

What must an officer do?

Each officer is expected to:

- acquire and keep up-to-date knowledge of work health and safety matters;
- gain an understanding of the nature of the operations of the business or undertaking of the department or authority and generally of the hazards and risks associated with those operations;

---

12   Interestingly, Ministers of a State or the Commonwealth are expressly excluded from the application of that definition. An elected member of a local authority is also excluded.

- ensure that the department or authority has available for use, and uses, appropriate resources and processes to enable hazards associated with the operations of the business or undertaking of the department or authority to be identified and risks associated with those hazards to be eliminated or minimised;
- ensure that the department or authority has appropriate processes for receiving and considering information regarding incidents, hazards and risks and responds in a timely way to that information;
- ensure that the department or authority has, and implements, processes for complying with any duty or obligation that it has under the model WHS Act; and
- verify the provision and use of the resources and processes referred to above.

Unlike the private sector, by and large, reporting structures and corporate governance processes in government departments may not address these requirements. The focus is often on briefings for Ministers and heads of departments on political issues that impact on the government of the day, or the status of the implementation of initiatives. The adoption of the types of corporate governance processes referred to in chapter 3 will require a shift in approach by the relevant departments or authorities.

Chapter

5

CHAPTER 6

WORKPLACE PARTICIPATION AND PROTECTION

Many people participate in work being done — those who are running the business in which the work is being done, those who supply things to enable the work to be done, and the workers who undertake the work activities. Those who require work to be done and those who carry out the work activity interact in many ways, both operationally and industrially. Often, they are each represented in those interactions.

This chapter looks at the promotion and regulation of that interaction in work health and safety matters, particularly through the role of elected health and safety representatives (HSRs), and through protection against discrimination and coercion.

The rationale for provisions relating to workplace participation

Why is consultation valuable?

The need for, and benefits of, consultation between an employer and employees has long been recognised. In is report on safety and health at work, the Robens Committee noted that:

> "... the promotion of safety and health at work is first and foremost a matter of efficient management. But it is not a management prerogative. In this context more than most, real progress is impossible without the full cooperation and commitment of all employees ...

> ... the involvement of employees in safety and health measures is too important for ... legislation to remain entirely silent on the matter.

> ... there should be a statutory duty on every employer to consult with his employees or their representatives at the workplace on the measures for promoting safety and health at work, and to provide arrangements for the participation of employees in the development of such measures ..."[1]

---

1   Robens, A (Lord), *Report of the committee on safety and health at work, 1970-1972* (Robens Report), London, Her Majesty's Stationery Office, 1972, pp 18 and 22.

Many studies have been undertaken and much literature deals with the benefits of, and processes for, consultation between workplace participants.[2]

Consultation with workers[3]

A person who is conducting a business or an undertaking (PCBU) owes duties of care and has other obligations under the model Work Health and Safety Act (model WHS Act). Those duties and obligations require PCBUs to make decisions that are relevant to health and safety risk management and legal compliance. They are accountable for health and safety outcomes and, while they should consult, they are not required to reach agreement with other workplace participants on the action that they take for compliance. There is, however, general recognition of the broad benefits of involvement in the decision-making processes of those PCBUs who are involved in undertaking the work activities.

Key managers of a PCBU will generally be aware of the circumstances in which work is to be done. They will be aware of the policies and procedures that direct or regulate the way in which the work is to be done, and they will generally be aware of the success or failure of those policies and procedures in protecting the health and safety of those carrying out the work activities. However, the reality in the workplace may differ from that which is understood by those decision-makers.

The circumstances in which work is being done, and the interactions between the various people involved in the work activities, may be subtly different from what is understood by the decision-makers. For example, there may be hazards and risks that are not known to those decision-makers. The workers may take practical steps to accommodate those different circumstances to allow them to undertake the work safely and without risks to health. Decisions made by or on behalf of a PCBU to alter the way in which the work is done, or the circumstances in which it is done, may not take these matters into account and may therefore fail to effectively provide for the elimination or minimisation of risks, and fail to provide legal compliance.

---

2   For further discussion on workplace OHS consultation, see CCH Editors, *Australian master OHS and environment guide* (2nd ed), Sydney, CCH Australia Limited, 2007, ch 6; Workplace Relations Ministers' Council, *National review into model occupational health and safety laws: second report to the Workplace Relations Ministers' Council* (Second Report), Canberra, WRMC, January 2009, ch 24; Johnstone, R, *Occupational health and safety law and policy*, Sydney, Law Book Company, 2004, ch 8; Maxwell, C, *Occupational Health and Safety Act review*, Melbourne, Victorian Department of Treasury and Finance, 2004, p 192; Hooker, R, *Review of the Occupational Safety and Health Act 1984: final report (WA)*, Perth, Department of Mines and Petroleum, 2006, p 96; Shaw, A, Blewett, V, Gunningham, N, Johnstone, R and Baker-Goldsmith, H, *Review of the NT Work Health Act and Mining Management Act: final report*, Darwin, 2007, p 105; and Brown, D and Hyam, S, *Review of workplace health and safety in Tasmania 2006: interim report*, Tasmania, Department of Justice, 2007, p 231.

3   For a discussion of the rationale for and benefits of consultation, see *Master OHS and environment guide*, op cit, at pp 87–89.

Effective communication between the representatives of a PCBU and those who are undertaking the work (through a process of consultation) allows the PCBU to make properly informed decisions which may, therefore, better provide for health and safety risk management and compliance.

Those who are undertaking the work must do so in accordance with the policies, procedures and instructions of the PCBU.[4] The policies, procedures and instructions will contain many elements that are directed at ensuring that the work is undertaken safely. Those elements may not directly contribute to achieving the work outcomes (for example, the manufacture of a product), and may even make the work process more difficult or slower. It is important that the workers understand the safety objectives of specific elements of policies, procedures and instructions. This can be achieved through communication between the PCBU and the workers.

Consultation with other duty holders

It is not only the workers who are undertaking the work who may have knowledge of relevant matters. Other PCBUs may be involved in the same work activities and, through that involvement, they may have information as to the circumstances in which the work will be done and they may have particular experience or expertise that may assist. They will be aware of how their activities may support or compromise those of others — and they will be aware of the health and safety implications. They need to know how the activities of other people may support or compromise their health and safety risk management activities.

Suppliers, those with management or control of the workplace, designers and others may also have relevant knowledge or require relevant knowledge. Therefore, they should be involved in the exchange of information relating to health and safety and in the making of decisions that affect health and safety.

Representation of workers

It may be inefficient and too time-consuming for a PCBU to consult with all affected workers individually, and it may be quite onerous, particularly where there are large numbers of affected workers. Consultation with all workers may also be ineffective, as there may be inconsistency between the information provided by the workers, and the information may be based on an erroneous understanding of the facts or technical matters. Workers may be reluctant to speak out on safety issues if they feel that there is a significant imbalance of power between themselves and the representatives of the PCBU.

---

4   Section 27 of the model WHS Act requires workers to comply with any reasonable instruction of a PCBU and any reasonable policy or procedure of the PCBU that has been notified to them.

The representation of workers in consultation with the PCBU may overcome these various concerns, and provide the following benefits:

- a single point of contact will provide greater efficiency;
- quality and usefulness of information through training and experience of that person through regular involvement in health and safety matters; and
- a representative, who has the support of the law, will feel that they have a right to be involved in consultations with the PCBU.

Union assistance and right of entry to a workplace

Unions have experience across many workplaces within an industry. The information that they obtain about health and safety matters through that experience may help workers and their representatives to identify whether the law has been complied with by a PCBU, to more effectively engage in consultation with a PCBU, and to effectively resolve issues relating to health and safety. When communicating with workers, a union may support the health and safety initiatives of a PCBU.[5]

An entitlement to enter the relevant workplace in order to consult and advise workers may assist a union in carrying out that function. As unions are third parties (that is, they are not entitled to enter a workplace other than by agreement of the person with management or control of the workplace or the PCBU, or as provided by other laws, for example, the *Fair Work Act 2009* (Cth)), OHS laws provide a right of entry.

As unions are otherwise involved in representing workers in industrial matters, the relationship between a union and a PCBU is often adversarial in nature — and not always based on trust and goodwill. The laws providing a right of entry of unions to a workplace for health and safety matters must be limited to provisions that are necessary for the health and safety role of a union, and must have limitations and safeguards against inappropriate conduct while at the workplace.

Under OHS laws, the right of entry is limited to the union's health and safety role, and limited to those who can effectively carry out that role. Union representatives who have been given a right to enter a workplace for health and safety matters should not be entitled to exercise coercive powers (given their adversarial role), as that may give rise to perceptions or fear of misuse that may result in mistrust and less effectiveness of the union representative when they are in consultation with a PCBU.

---

5   For a discussion of the benefits of involving unions in work health and safety matters, see pp 383–384 of the Second Report and the resources referred to in the footnotes.

Providing representatives with powers

If workers believe that a serious health or safety issue is not being properly dealt with by a PCBU, they may feel the need for early intervention in the workplace. While inspectors of the regulator may intervene, there are limited numbers of them and they must necessarily take time to travel to workplaces. The relevant issue may also be too serious and urgent to await the arrival of an inspector. Health and safety representatives are therefore given powers to ensure the ongoing safety of workers. Those powers may be used to direct the PCBU to undertake specific activities or provide specific measures to make the work or processes safe and without risks to health, or to require that work ceases until it can be undertaken safely and without risks to health.

Exercising those powers may remove the need to involve inspectors at the workplace, and resolving these matters by the workplace participants may promote ongoing consultation and cooperation — and allow the resources of the regulator to be used elsewhere.

As the exercise of these powers may have serious consequences for the PCBU and others, they should only be able to be exercised in limited and quite specific circumstances, and be subject to review.

Issue resolution

A PCBU (directly or through its representatives) and workers may not always agree on health and safety matters. This may occur as a result of one or both having incomplete or inaccurate information. However, many concerns about health and safety may be resolved through discussions between the affected workers and the representative of the PCBU most directly involved with the work. Where such discussions fail to resolve concerns or disputes about health and safety and what should be done about them, OHS laws should encourage the parties to follow processes that provide for a timely and effective resolution of the issue.

Protection against discrimination, misrepresentation and coercion

The effective management of health and safety is supported by the involvement of all who contribute to work being done, directly or through their representatives — and being involved in health and safety roles and activities should be promoted, not discouraged. Occupational health and safety laws should accordingly support such involvement, and prohibit conduct which is adverse to that involvement or its effectiveness.

The exercise of powers or rights by a worker or an HSR may cause disruption to operations or require costs to be incurred by a PCBU. They may also inconvenience other workers or other parties. A duty holder may be subjected to regulator intervention, enforcement activities or prosecution because of the involvement of a person who is assisting in an investigation or other activity of a regulator. By complying with the laws and recognising the benefits of doing so, a PCBU will cooperate with and engage effectively with worker representatives and inspectors, and be involved in the investigation of health and safety matters. It is important that all of these parties are encouraged to be involved in the processes provided in the OHS laws in order to support the elimination and minimisation of health and safety risks. The law must support that involvement by protecting those parties from adverse action being taken against them. That is, the law must deter parties from being "punished" for their involvement in health and safety matters or for performing functions and exercising powers under the laws.

Similarly, the law should prohibit conduct that coerces people into taking unsafe action, or that prevents them from taking action regarding health and safety matters.

The rights, powers and obligations of parties are found in provisions that may be considered by some to be complex and that may not be fully known or understood. The law should prohibit the misrepresentation of powers, rights or obligations, as that may result in action not being taken that is necessary for health and safety, or action being taken that is contrary to the interests of health and safety.

Consultation, cooperation and coordination between duty holders

What is required

The model laws recognise the benefits (referred to earlier in this chapter) of a PCBU engaging effectively with others who are involved in the work activities, or providing the things that are necessary for this to occur. Section 45 of the model WHS Act provides:

> "If more than one person has a duty in respect of the same matter under this Act, each person with the duty must, so far as is reasonably practicable, consult, cooperate and coordinate activities with all other persons who have a duty in relation to the same matter."

This duty, which will be referred to as "horizontal engagement", reflects the views of the Panel that undertook the national review into model OHS laws (see recommendations 2(f) and 98).[6]

---

6   See Workplace Relations Ministers' Council, *National review into model occupational health and safety laws: first report to the Workplace Relations Ministers' Council* (First Report), Canberra, WRMC, October 2008, para 4.47; and Second Report, para 24.27.

The relationship between horizontal engagement and other duties and obligations

Identifying the link between the duty for horizontal engagement and the duties of care and other obligations is a key to understanding this requirement. As discussed below, the model laws change the duty of an employer to consult employees to the duty of a PCBU to consult workers, thereby requiring that all who are actively involved in determining how work is done, and in doing the work, engage in a meaningful exchange of information. The duty placed on a PCBU for horizontal engagement with other duty holders is simply an extension of this concept.

The primary duty of care requires a PCBU to ensure various outcomes and activities, so far as is reasonably practicable, in the conduct of its business or undertaking. There may be more than one PCBU with the primary duty of care in relation to the same activity (for example, contractors, labour hire staff, occupiers and/or suppliers). Primary duty holders need not undertake the particular activities themselves, and may comply with the primary duty by ensuring that some other duty holder does so (but will breach the duty if they do not ensure that this occurs). The duty of a PCBU for horizontal engagement is intended to encourage concurrent duty holders to work together to ensure that the required measures are taken in order to produce the required health and safety outcomes.

An officer will owe a duty to exercise due diligence to ensure that the relevant body complies with its duties and obligations. It is clear that meeting the due diligence requirements (as defined in the model WHS Act) will require consultation with others within the organisation and the coordination of activities (for example, conducting investigations and audits, reporting, and so on) with other officers and with workers.

Workers are required to comply with reasonable policies, procedures and instructions as part of their duty of care. The duty of a PCBU to cooperate with other duty holders is consistent with this, and the proper engagement of workers when consulting with a PCBU is essential to the effectiveness of that process.

The parties involved in a health and safety issue will be required to make reasonable efforts to achieve a timely, final and effective resolution of the issue. Agreed or default procedures for doing so will apply. The obligation to consult and cooperate clearly supports the issue resolution requirements. It is clear, therefore, that compliance by a PCBU with the duty for horizontal engagement is necessary for the PCBU and others to be compliant with various duties and obligations under the model laws. Compliance with each of these duties and obligations is a key consideration when determining the detail of the required consultation, cooperation and coordination of activities.

Practical compliance

What is required to meet the duty for horizontal engagement will depend on the circumstances. The following questions provide a useful process for determining what should be done:

- What is the relevant activity or issue?
- What duty or obligation do I have in relation to that activity?
- What do I need to know to ensure that I meet the duty?
- Who else is involved in the activity?
- How may each of us affect health or safety in relation to that activity?
- Where do our activities intersect with those of others, and where do we each compromise, or support, the health and safety activities of the other?
- What steps should I therefore take to ensure that we communicate and work together effectively for the protection of health and safety?

Compliance with the duty for horizontal engagement (and the duties of care) cannot be ensured without considering these issues.

The duty for horizontal engagement is subject to the qualifier of what is reasonably practicable (which is defined in s 17 of the model WHS Act, as it applies to "ensuring health or safety"). To the extent that it is relevant, the definition of "reasonably practicable" and the elements referred to in it are applicable to the duty for horizontal engagement. The list of considerations in that definition is inclusive, not exclusive, and all relevant matters in the circumstances must be considered.

Compliance with the duty for horizontal engagement should be determined by achieving outcomes rather than following processes. For consultation, this means considering the amount of consultation that is necessary to achieve an effective exchange of information in the circumstances. The urgency of the issue, the availability of people, the seriousness of the risk, and the information obtained during consultation will all be relevant to how much consultation is required.[7]

For the cooperation and coordination of activities with other duty holders, this will mean doing what is reasonably necessary to ensure that the activities of the PCBU and other duty holders for work health and safety risk management and compliance support each other and work effectively together, without gaps or inconsistencies.

Implications

The duty for horizontal engagement by a PCBU with other duty holders is a new feature in OHS laws, introduced by the model WHS Act. A PCBU will need to

---

7   These points are discussed at para 24.25–4.26 of the Second Report. See also Sherriff, B, *OHS in practice: a guide to legislation in Victoria*, Melbourne, Anstat, 2005, pp 4-7 and 4-8.

ensure that they have policies and procedures in place to provide for compliance with this duty. Those policies and procedures may be supported by appropriate provisions in agreements with other duty holders, and will need to be supported by practical measures for monitoring and verifying that the relevant activities are undertaken and are effective.

A PCBU will need to identify those people who have a duty of care in relation to the same matter (for example, the work activity, the provision of plant for use at the workplace, and so on), consult with them to ensure an effective exchange of information necessary for each to comply with their duties and obligations, and ensure that their respective activities are coordinated. This will need to occur prior to, at the commencement of, and throughout the involvement of each in the relevant matter.

Consultation with workers

Who must consult and with whom[8]

The model WHS Act requires a PCBU, so far as is reasonably practicable, to consult with workers who carry out work for their business or undertaking, and who are, or are likely to be, directly affected by a matter relating to health or safety at work. The obligation is accordingly on a PCBU to undertake the consultation. However, it should be noted that a worker's duty of care[9] requires a worker to comply with any reasonable policy or procedure of the PCBU relating to work health or safety that has been notified to workers (which may properly include procedures relating to consultation). Also, the model laws require an HSR to consult the PCBU before exercising powers to issue a provisional improvement notice or to direct a cessation of work.

The PCBU must consult the workers who are directly affected by the relevant health or safety matter. The broad definition of a worker extends beyond the direct employees of the PCBU to include any person who carries out work in any capacity for the PCBU. The PCBU must accordingly consult with contractors and subcontractors and their employees, labour hire personnel, volunteers, and any other people who are working within the business or undertaking and who are affected by the relevant matter.

This means that there may be more than one PCBU who is required to consult with specific workers in respect of a particular health and safety matter. That process of consultation should be coordinated, as is required by the duty for horizontal engagement noted above.

Chapter

6

---

8   For a discussion of this issue, see pp 106–107 of the Second Report.
9   Model WHS Act, s 27.

What is required

The model WHS Act sets out what is required when undertaking consultation, including:

1. relevant information about the matter must be shared with the workers;
2. workers must be given a reasonable opportunity:
   a. to express their views and to raise work health and safety issues in relation to the matter; and
   b. to contribute to the decision-making process relating to the matter;
3. the views of workers must be taken into account by the PCBU; and
4. the workers who are being consulted must be advised of the outcome of the consultation in a timely manner.

The model laws also provide that, where workers are represented by an HSR, the consultation must involve that representative.

If a PCBU and the workers have agreed to procedures for consultation, the consultation must be undertaken in accordance with those procedures (which must be consistent with s 47 of the model WHS Act). Such procedures may provide for consultation only with an HSR of the workers, with an HSR and workers, through a health and safety committee (HSC), or by other means.

When consultation must occur

Section 48 of the model WHS Act provides that consultation is required in respect of the following health and safety matters:

1. when identifying hazards and assessing risks arising from the work carried out or to be carried out by the business or undertaking;
2. when making decisions about ways to eliminate or minimise those risks;
3. when making decisions about the adequacy of facilities for the welfare of workers;
4. when proposing changes that may affect the health or safety of workers;
5. when making decisions about the procedures for:
   a. resolving the work health or safety issues;
   b. monitoring the health of workers;
   c. monitoring the conditions at any workplace under the management or control of the PCBU;
   d. providing information and training for workers; or
   e. consulting with workers; and

6. when carrying out any other activity that is prescribed by the regulations for the purposes of s 48.

The model laws, therefore, clearly identify specific matters in respect of which consultation must occur. A PCBU need not consult with workers or their representatives on other health and safety matters. However, that is not to suggest that a PCBU should not appropriately consult on matters that are not listed above. It may be necessary for a PCBU to consult on other matters to ensure that they have sufficient information to enable them to comply with their duties of care or other obligations.

Point (5) above refers to decisions about procedures for the various matters listed in (a) to (e), but consultation is not required when those particular matters are being dealt with. However, a PCBU may find it useful to consult when undertaking those matters.

The extent to which a PCBU should consult with workers may be relevant when determining the reasonableness of the PCBU's policies, procedures or instructions (in order to determine workers' compliance with their duty of care).

The standard of reasonably practicable

The qualifier "reasonably practicable" is defined in s 17 of the model WHS Act (as it applies to "ensuring health or safety"). While the process of consultation is part of an overall process for ensuring health or safety, the definition of reasonably practicable may not apply to consultation. However, the approach set out in the definition and the elements of it may be quite relevant to consultation — particularly the part of the definition that refers to what "is, or was, at a particular time, reasonably able to be done".

What is reasonably practicable in relation to consultation is likely to be considered by the regulators and courts to reflect what measures are able to be taken for consultation and the degree to which the taking of such measures is reasonably required. The following are suggested as relevant considerations:

- the more severe or likely the potential outcomes to be avoided or minimised through consultation, the more effort may reasonably be required in that consultation;
- the need for a timely response may limit the extent of the consultation that is reasonably required;
- the availability of people to be consulted (for example, an HSR), when combined with other factors, will be relevant to determining the extent of the consultation that is required; and

Chapter

6

- where consultation is undertaken directly with workers, rather than or in addition to their HSR, the absence of new information from ongoing consultation may render further consultation unnecessary.

These are just some of the considerations, and the circumstances will determine what consultation can occur and the extent to which it may reasonably be required.[10]

How this differs from current laws

Provisions in the model WHS Act relating to consultation between a PCBU and workers are closely modelled on the current provisions in Victoria.[11] There are consultation obligations to similar effect in other jurisdictions, but not all. This duty will accordingly only be new, and require change, in those jurisdictions whose current laws do not include this duty, or do not provide the level of detail as to the circumstances in which consultation must occur.

Issue resolution

The model WHS Act recognises the benefits of the timely and effective resolution of work health and safety issues by requiring work participants to engage in processes to achieve that outcome. However, in recognising the need for flexibility and for issue resolution procedures to meet the specific needs of the workplace and work participants, the model laws do not prescribe in detail the processes to be followed.

The parties to issue resolution

The model WHS Act identifies the following people as the parties to a work health and safety issue that is required to be resolved in accordance with the Act:

- each PCBU who is involved in the issue, or their representative;
- the HSR of a work group of workers affected by the issue; and
- if the workers are not in a work group, then the workers or their representative.

A PCBU is required to try to resolve an issue with an HSR (where there is one), rather than with the workers directly.

A representative of a PCBU must be a person who is not an HSR, and is a person who has an appropriate level of seniority and is sufficiently competent to act as the representative of the PCBU.

---

10   These points are discussed at para 24.25–24.26 of the Second Report. See also Sherriff, op cit, at pp 4-7 and 4-8; and *Master OHS and environment guide*, op cit, at pp 103–105.

11   *Occupational Health and Safety Act 2004* (Vic), s 35 and 36.

Issues to be resolved in accordance with the model WHS Act

The issue resolution provisions of the model WHS Act will apply:

> "… if a matter about work health and safety arises at a workplace or from the conduct of a business or undertaking and the matter is not resolved after discussion between the parties to the issue."[12]

The intention of this provision is to encourage the relevant workplace participants (for example, an affected worker and their immediate supervisor or manager) to first discuss a concern or health and safety matter before involving other parties or undertaking a more formal process. That is, an "issue" only arises after discussions identify that there is an ongoing concern or dispute.[13] This does not mean that an HSR or a representative of a PCBU is excluded from those preliminary discussions — only that it is not necessary that they be involved in those discussions. The entitlement of a worker to obtain the assistance and representation of their elected HSR is not removed or limited by this provision.

The process for issue resolution

The model WHS Act requires the parties to issue resolution to make reasonable efforts to achieve a timely, final and effective resolution of the issue. This must be undertaken in accordance with an agreed procedure or, if there is no agreed procedure, the default procedure prescribed in the regulations.

A representative of a party to an issue may enter the workplace to engage in discussions, with a view to assisting the resolution of the issue. This may include a representative of a relevant union or industry association, or another person who is formally representing one of the parties to the issue.

If an issue has not been resolved after reasonable efforts have been made, a party to the issue may ask the regulator to appoint an inspector to attend the workplace to assist in resolving the issue. Such a request does not prevent a worker from exercising their right to cease unsafe work, or prevent an HSR from issuing a provisional improvement notice or a direction to cease unsafe work.

When attending the workplace to assist in the resolution of an issue, an inspector may exercise any of their compliance powers, such as the issuing of a notice. Action taken by an inspector at the workplace in respect of the issue may be subject to review,[14] providing for a formal determination of the issue by the regulator or (ultimately) by the relevant court or tribunal.

Chapter

6

---

12 Model WHS Act, s 80(1).
13 For a discussion of this, see pp 168–169 of the Second Report; and Sherriff, op cit, at pp 7-53 and 7-54.
14 Under Part 12 of the model WHS Act.

How this differs from current laws

Current OHS laws in all Australian jurisdictions provide for issue resolution, but with some differences as to detail. The provisions in the model WHS Act are based on those found in the Victorian *Occupational Health and Safety Act 2004*, but they only provide details regarding who is to be a party to an issue, the objective of a timely and effective resolution of an issue, and the issue resolution process to be provided in agreed or default procedures. The extent to which the issue resolution requirements will differ from those currently in place in a particular jurisdiction will depend on the default procedures, the details of which will be provided in the regulations.

Worker representation

Determining who will be represented

The model WHS Act provides for the representation of workers. The broad definition of workers not only includes the direct employees of a PCBU, but also other people who are undertaking work in the business or undertaking. The workers who are entitled to be represented may therefore be employees of more than one PCBU, or may be volunteers or other people who are not in employment.

The aim of representing workers is to facilitate consultation and the resolution of issues in relation to work health and safety. The representatives are the conduit for the flow of information between a PCBU (and their representatives) and the workers. To adequately fulfil this role, representatives of workers should be familiar with the environment in which the workers work, the work undertaken by them, and the risks and hazards to which they are exposed.

The model laws adopt the approach taken in the Victorian *Occupational Health and Safety Act 2004* for identifying who an HSR will represent. Workers who are working within a business or an undertaking are grouped into work groups, with each work group being represented by a member of the work group. The numbers of work groups, and the workers who are part of a work group, are to be determined by negotiation and agreement between the PCBU and the workers. The negotiations will determine the number and composition of the work groups, the number of HSRs and deputy HSRs, and the workplace or workplaces to which the work groups will apply.

It may be appropriate for a work group to comprise workers who are undertaking work at more than one workplace. As workers may be undertaking work for more than one PCBU (for example, for a labour on-hirer and a host), it may also be appropriate for a work group to apply to more than one business or undertaking. If negotiations fail, an inspector may be appointed for the purposes of making a determination on the number and composition of work groups. Multiple business work groups and multiple workplace work groups can only be determined by agreement.

The model WHS Act does not set out the factors that should be taken into consideration when determining the composition of a work group.[15] However, the parties, and any inspector who has been called in to determine a work group, should consider which workers may be conveniently represented by a person who would have an appropriate understanding of the work undertaken by them, and be readily accessible to those workers. The matters to be taken into account under s 46 of the Victorian *Occupational Health and Safety Act 2004* are directed at these considerations and include (any references to "employees" have been replaced with "workers"):

1. the number of workers at the workplace or workplaces;
2. the nature of each type of work performed at the workplace or workplaces;
3. the number and grouping of workers who perform the same or similar types of work, or who work under the same or similar arrangements;
4. the areas at the workplace or workplaces where each type of work is performed;
5. the nature of any hazards at the workplace or workplaces;
6. any overtime or shift working arrangements at the workplace or workplaces; and
7. whether other languages are spoken by the workers.

Determining the representatives

As it is the workers who will be represented by the HSR, it is they who are entitled to elect one of the members of their work group as an HSR. Unless disqualified from being entitled to be elected, each member of the work group is entitled to be elected. Each member of the work group is entitled to vote.

The procedure by which an HSR will be elected is a matter for the workers in the work group to determine. The relevant PCBU must provide any resources, facilities and assistance that are reasonably necessary or are prescribed by the regulations to enable an election to be conducted. The election may be conducted with the assistance of a union, or other person or organisation, if a majority of the workers in the work group so determines. The PCBU may assist in the election, but only if a majority of the members of the work group wishes them to do so.

Deputy HSRs may also be elected, if that is the outcome of the negotiation between the PCBU and the workers. The election of a deputy HSR provides for ongoing representation when the elected HSR is unavailable.

Chapter

6

---

15 Unlike s 46 of the *Occupational and Safety Act 2004* (Vic).

Powers and functions of HSRs

The model WHS Act gives a broad range of powers and functions to HSRs, all of which are aimed at one or more of:

- facilitating effective consultation and issue resolution;
- monitoring the compliance of the PCBU;
- investigating complaints from members of the work group relating to work health and safety; and
- inquiring into risks to the health or safety of workers in the work group arising from the conduct of the business or undertaking.

To facilitate these outcomes, an HSR is entitled to:

- inspect the workplace (or part of the workplace) at which a worker in the work group works at any time, after giving reasonable notice to the PCBU or immediately in the event of an incident or a situation involving a serious risk to the health or safety of a person emanating from an immediate or imminent exposure to a hazard;
- accompany an inspector during an inspection of the workplace (or a part of the workplace) at which a worker in the work group works;
- with the consent of a worker or a group of workers, be present at an interview between an inspector and a PCBU concerning work health and safety;
- request the establishment of an HSC; and
- receive information concerning the work health and safety of workers in the work group.

The powers and functions of an HSR are ordinarily limited to the particular work group that they have been elected to represent. However, they may exercise their powers and perform functions in respect of another work group, *if* there is a serious risk to health or safety emanating from an immediate or imminent exposure to a hazard that affects or may affect a member of that other work group, *and if* a member of that work group asks for the assistance *and* the HSR for that other work group is found (after reasonable enquiry) to be unavailable.

An HSR may, whenever necessary, request the assistance of any person, and it may be necessary for that other person to enter the workplace to provide that assistance. The PCBU must allow that other person to have access to the workplace if this is necessary to enable the assistance to be provided, but need not do so if the person assisting has had their workplace health and safety entry permit revoked or suspended, or if the person is disqualified from holding such an entry permit.

The PCBU may refuse to grant workplace access to a person who is assisting an HSR on "reasonable grounds". It is unclear what "reasonable grounds" will be, but they will be determined by reference to the particular circumstances. Past misconduct of the person assisting, a lack of technical knowledge or relevant experience such that they are not able to assist the representative (to assist, they must add to the ability of the HSR to undertake the relevant activity), or the presence of hazards at the workplace such that there is a serious risk to the health or safety of a person entering it may all be considered to be reasonable grounds.

The model WHS Act provides that an HSR may issue a provisional improvement notice if the HSR has formed a reasonable belief that a person is contravening a provision of the Act, or has done so and is likely to do so in the future. The notice may require the person (for example, a PCBU) to remedy the contravention, prevent it from occurring, or remedy the things or operations causing the contravention. The notice, unless it is the subject of a review by an inspector called in for that purpose, has the same effect as a notice issued by an inspector, with the same consequences for failing to comply with it.

An HSR must not issue a provisional improvement notice unless they have first consulted with the person to whom it is issued. Also, an HSR must not issue a provisional improvement notice unless they have undertaken the necessary training. Significantly, the model WHS Act provides that an HSR may make minor changes to, or cancel, a provisional improvement notice. This should be a useful improvement to current laws, as it avoids the need to seek a review of a notice if the parties agree to its modification or cancellation.

An HSR may direct a worker in the work group that they represent to cease work if they have a reasonable concern that to carry out the work would expose the worker to a serious risk to the worker's health or safety (emanating from an immediate or imminent exposure to a hazard). The HSR must first consult with the PCBU (unless the risk is so serious that it is not reasonable to do so) and attempt to resolve the issue under the issue resolution provisions of the model WHS Act. The power of an HSR to direct that unsafe work ceases is consistent with the right of a worker to cease that unsafe work.

As indicated earlier in this chapter, an elected HSR is entitled to be involved in consultation with a PCBU, on behalf of the affected workers, and be involved in the resolution of issues.

The model laws include procedural requirements for issuing notices, for HSR training, for workers to undertake alternative work if they cease unsafe work, and for the contents of provisional improvement notices to be displayed.

A PCBU is required to take various steps to facilitate the effective exercise by an HSR of their functions and powers. The obligations of the PCBU include:[16]

---

16   Model WHS Act, s 69, subject to limitations on the obligations of a PCBU set out in s 70 of the Act.

- consulting and conferring with the HSR on the various matters that are set out in s 69 of the model WHS Act;
- allowing the HSR to attend interviews;
- providing resources, facilities and assistance to enable the HSR to exercise their powers or perform their functions;
- allowing people assisting the HSR to have access to the workplace; and
- providing prescribed training.[17]

To support the function of an HSR, a PCBU will be required to provide workers with an "HSR information statement" that has been prepared by the regulator and which provides details about the powers, functions and entitlements of HSRs under the model laws.

Health and safety committees

The model WHS Act includes the provisions commonly found in OHS laws for establishing a health and safety committee (HSC) for a business or an undertaking or a part of it. This must occur within two months after being requested to do so by an HSR, or by five or more workers at the workplace, or if required by regulation to do so. A PCBU may establish an HSC on their own initiative.

The model laws provide for the constitution of an HSC, including that at least half of the members of the HSC must be workers who are not nominated by the PCBU, and for there to be HSRs on the committee. The functions of an HSC are:

1. to facilitate cooperation between the PCBU and workers in instigating, developing and carrying out measures designed to ensure the workers' health and safety at work;
2. to assist in developing standards, rules and procedures relating to health and safety that are to be followed or complied with at the workplace; and
3. such other functions as are prescribed by the regulations or agreed to by the PCBU and the HSC.

Other than providing that an HSC must meet at least once every three months and at any reasonable time at the request of at least half of the members of the committee, the model WHS Act does not provide any requirements for or direction on the way in which an HSC may operate. That is a matter for the committee to determine.

How this differs from current laws

The laws relating to the representation of workers vary in the Australian jurisdictions. The provisions of the model WHS Act relating to HSRs and HSCs are closely modelled on those in the Victorian *Occupational Health and Safety Act 2004*.

---

17   See s 71 of the model WHS Act for details of the training and determining arrangements for it.

The process of determining a work group or work groups will be new in some jurisdictions. The provisions relating to the election of HSRs will be less detailed than in some jurisdictions (for example, Queensland). The entitlement of an HSR to issue a provisional improvement notice (or an equivalent) does not currently exist in New South Wales or Tasmania, and has only recently been introduced in Queensland.

While the right of a worker to cease unsafe work exists at common law, the specific provision of this right in the model WHS Act will be new in many jurisdictions. The right of an HSR to direct that unsafe work ceases currently only exists in Victoria, South Australia, the Northern Territory and the Commonwealth. That right will therefore be new in all other jurisdictions.

There are many changes in detail that will apply in the different jurisdictions under the model laws. These may be identified by cross-referring the detail provided above and set out in the model WHS Act with the information contained in the various tables in the Second Report.[18]

Union rights of entry

Earlier in this chapter, the role that a union may play in representing or advising a worker or an HSR on work health and safety matters was discussed. For that purpose, a union representative may need to access the workplace for the purposes of discussions with the relevant worker or HSR, or to view relevant parts of the workplace, plant or systems of work.

Current OHS laws provide for the right of a union representative to enter a workplace for specific work health and safety purposes, in addition to rights of entry provided under industrial laws. The model laws also provide for union rights of entry.

Qualifications for entitlement to exercise entry powers

Not every union member or official is entitled to exercise a right of entry to a workplace under the model WHS Act. Only a work health and safety entry permit (WHS entry permit) holder may enter a workplace for the purposes provided in the model WHS Act and exercise the rights provided in the Act.

---

18   See the following tables from the Second Report: Table 31 at p 486 (consultation, participation and representation); Table 33 at p 119 (provision of work groups); Table 34 at p 124 (election of HSRs); Table 35 at p 492 (HSR duties and functions); Table 36 at p 496 (employers' obligations to HSRs); Table 37 at p 141 (provision of training for HSRs); Table 39 at p 153 (establishment of HSCs); and Tables 40 and 41 at p 178 (cessation of unsafe work).

A union[19] may apply to the authorising authority for the issue of a WHS entry permit to a person who is a union official. That person must satisfactorily complete prescribed training, and also hold an entry permit under the *Fair Work Act 2009* (Cth) or the relevant State or Territory industrial law. The model WHS Act includes detailed provisions for the making of, and consideration of an application for, a WHS entry permit. The model laws also provide for a person to be disqualified from obtaining a permit, and for imposing conditions on, suspending or revoking a permit.

The requirements and processes for entry

A WHS entry permit holder may only seek entry under the model WHS Act for specified purposes relating to a worker who is a member or eligible to be a member of the relevant union, whose industrial interests at the workplace the relevant union is entitled to represent, and who works at that workplace.

Entry may be made to a workplace for the following purposes:

- to enquire into a suspected contravention of the model WHS Act that relates to or affects a relevant worker;
- the WHS entry permit holder must reasonably suspect that the contravention has occurred or is occurring before entering the workplace; and
- to consult with and advise relevant workers who wish to participate in discussions on work health and safety matters.

A WHS entry permit holder may enter a workplace immediately to enquire into a suspected contravention but must, as soon as is reasonably practicable after entering the workplace, give notice of the entry and the suspected contravention to the relevant PCBU(s) (unless giving the notice would defeat the purpose of the entry or unreasonably delay the permit holder in an urgent case).

It is likely that the regulations will require (as is the current position in Victoria) the WHS entry permit holder to provide specific details of the particular section of the model WHS Act that is being contravened, and how that section is being contravened (for example, a contravention of s 18(1) and (3)(a) by failing to ensure the provision of safe systems of work for the carrying out of a specified activity).

A WHS entry permit holder must give written notice of their intended entry to consult and advise workers at least 24 hours but not more than 14 days before the entry, unless the permit holder has, under s 487(1)(b) of the *Fair Work Act 2009* (Cth), given notice to the PCBU of the entry to hold discussions with workers.

---

19   As defined in s 4 of the model WHS Act, being an employee organisation registered under the *Fair Work (Registered Organisations) Act 2009* (Cth) or registered or recognised as an association of employees or independent contractors under a State or Territory industrial law.

While immediate entry may be made to inquire into a suspected contravention (which may deal with a serious and immediate or imminent risk), entry to a workplace for the purposes of consultation and advice to workers is aligned to the provisions of the *Fair Work Act 2009* (Cth).

On entry, the WHS entry permit holder must present for examination, on request, a photograph and entry permit. A WHS entry permit holder may only enter a workplace during usual working hours, and must not enter any part of a workplace that is used only for residential purposes.

Powers on entry

A WHS entry permit holder may, on entering a workplace to enquire into a suspected contravention:

1. inspect any work system, plant, substance, structure or other thing that is relevant to a suspected contravention;

2. consult with the relevant workers in relation to the suspected contravention;

3. consult with the PCBU about the suspected contravention;

4. require the relevant PCBU to allow the permit holder to inspect, and make copies of, any document that is directly relevant to the suspected contravention that is kept at the workplace or is accessible from a computer that is kept at the workplace; and

5. warn any person whom the permit holder reasonably believes is exposed to a serious risk to their health or safety (emanating from an immediate or imminent exposure to a hazard).[20]

Although a WHS entry permit holder may immediately enter a workplace to inquire into a suspected contravention, the permit holder must give at least 24 hours' notice before entering for the purposes of inspecting or making copies of certain documents that are directly relevant to a suspected contravention.

A WHS entry permit holder may exercise a right of entry to a workplace only in respect of the area of the workplace where the relevant workers work, or any other work area that directly affects the health and safety of those workers. Provisions of the *Fair Work Act 2009* (Cth) that limit the times during which consultation and advice may occur, and where they may occur within a workplace, are not included in the model WHS Act.

Breaches relating to entry

The right of entry of a WHS entry permit holder is supported by prohibitions against a person who is refusing or delaying the entry of a WHS entry permit holder

Chapter

6

---

20   Model WHS Act, s 117(1).

without reasonable excuse.[21] A person must not intentionally and unreasonably hinder a WHS entry permit holder in, or obstruct them from, entering a workplace or exercising any rights at a workplace.

The model WHS Act provides for the following breaches by a WHS entry permit holder:

- intentionally and unreasonably delaying, hindering or obstructing any person, disrupting any work at a workplace, or otherwise acting in an improper manner; and

- using or disclosing information or a document obtained in the exercise of entry powers for a purpose that is not related to the enquiry or the rectifying of the suspected contravention, unless the permit holder reasonably believes that the use or disclosure is necessary to lessen or prevent a serious risk to a person's health or safety or to public health or safety, or the disclosure is a necessary part of an investigation or other legal process noted in the model laws.

A WHS entry permit holder must not exercise a right of entry to a workplace under the model WHS Act unless that person complies with any reasonable request by a relevant PCBU to comply with any work health and safety requirement that applies to the workplace, and any other legislated requirement that applies to that type of workplace. This is relevant to the reasonableness of a PCBU or other person refusing or delaying entry to a workplace, or hindering or obstructing the WHS entry permit holder, and to the potential breach of a permit holder of acting in "an improper manner".

Right of entry breaches are not offences, but may be subject to civil penalties.

Resolution of disputes relating to entry

Any party to a dispute relating to the entitlement of a WHS entry permit holder to enter a workplace, or relating to the conduct of the permit holder or any other person during the course of that entry, may be referred to an inspector to resolve. The authorising authority[22] may deal with a dispute about a right of entry under the model WHS Act, and may do so in any manner it thinks fit (including by means of mediation, conciliation or arbitration).

How this differs from current laws

The majority of OHS Acts confer powers on authorised union representatives to enter workplaces for health and safety purposes. There are, however, marked

---

21 A reasonable excuse, for example, may be that it is unsafe to enter the relevant part of the workplace.

22 The body that deals with applications for WHS entry permits, or the suspension, revocation or other action in relation to them.

differences between the jurisdictions on the processes for entry, purposes for entry, and rights on entry.[23] Some jurisdictions provide for a right of entry to enquire into or investigate a suspected contravention, but do not provide for entry to consult and advise workers. Other jurisdictions permit entry for the purpose of discussing OHS issues. Each of these purposes will be provided for by the model WHS Act.

The model laws broaden the circumstances in which a union representative may enter a workplace for health and safety purposes and, in most jurisdictions, provide enlarged powers on entry. The model laws effectively provide for an amalgamation of existing right of entry provisions. However, unlike current provisions, breaches of right of entry provisions will not be offences and therefore do not give rise to a criminal conviction. Breaches may result in civil penalties being imposed.

Implications

People who are conducting a business or an undertaking will need to become familiar with the details of the right of entry provisions and ensure that they and WHS entry permit holders comply strictly with those provisions. A failure to do so may lead to proceedings being taken for a civil penalty. Work health and safety entry permit holders should also ensure that they and any relevant PCBU or other person comply strictly with the right of entry provisions.

It is likely that disputes will continue to arise in relation to the purposes of the right of entry and the conduct of the WHS entry permit holder, the PCBU or other person. The role of the regulator and its inspectors will be critical to ensuring the effectiveness of these provisions.

Protection against discrimination, misrepresentation and coercion

The model WHS Act provides various means by which people may be involved in promoting and securing health and safety in the workplace. The Act provides for the roles of HSRs, HSCs, workers, WHS entry permit holders and inspectors in processes of consultation, issue resolution, risk management and inquiry or investigation into suspected breaches of the laws. Workers are also entitled to cease unsafe work.

The exercise of powers or rights may cause disruption to operations or require costs to be incurred by the PCBU or others. However, the roles and the exercise of powers and rights of each party must be supported by the model WHS Act prohibiting conduct which is adverse to that involvement or its effectiveness. That is, the model WHS Act deters parties from being "punished" for their involvement

---

23   The current arrangements are identified in Table 67 on pp 378–379 of the Second Report.

in health and safety matters or for performing functions or exercising powers under the model laws.

What is unlawful discrimination?

The model WHS Act provides that a person is engaging in unlawful discriminatory conduct if, for a prohibited reason, the person:

- dismisses a worker;
- terminates a contract for services with a worker;
- puts a worker to their detriment in the engagement of the worker;
- alters the position of a worker to the worker's detriment;
- refuses or fails to engage a prospective worker;
- treats a prospective worker less favourably than another prospective worker would be treated in offering terms of engagement;
- terminates a commercial arrangement with a person; and
- refuses or fails to enter into a commercial arrangement with a person.

Consistent with the broadening of duties and obligations beyond the employment relationship, these provisions of the model WHS Act refer to a worker or prospective worker, rather than an employee or prospective employee. The provisions go further to extend into commercial arrangements. The provisions are clearly intended to make discriminatory conduct, for a prohibited reason, unlawful against any person in the course of a relationship associated with work.

The prohibited reasons are those which are connected with the involvement of a person who is undertaking a role under the model WHS Act, or of a person who cooperates with or assists another person who is undertaking a role under the Act. These roles include:

- being or exercising powers or performing functions as an HSR or as a member of an HSC;
- performing a particular function under the model WHS Act, or performing a function under the Act in a particular way;
- assisting or proposing to assist or give information to any person who is exercising a power or function under the model WHS Act;
- raising or proposing to raise an issue or concern about work health or safety with a PCBU, an inspector, a WHS entry permit holder, an HSR, a member of an HSC, or another worker or any other person who has a duty under the model WHS Act or is exercising a power or performing a function under the Act;
- being involved in or proposing to be involved in resolving a work health or safety issue; and

- taking action or proposing to take action to seek compliance by any person with a duty or an obligation under the model WHS Act.

A person only commits an offence for discriminatory conduct if the proscribed reason was the *dominant* reason for the discriminatory conduct (that is, it was for that reason more than any other reason that the person engaged in the discriminatory conduct). Civil proceedings in relation to discriminatory conduct may only be brought if the proscribed reason was a *substantial* reason for the conduct. The model laws also make it clear that it is an offence for a person to request, instruct, induce, encourage, authorise or assist another person to engage in discriminatory conduct.

Prohibition of coercion or inducement

There may be circumstances in which a person is not subjected to adverse action of the kinds referred to in the definition of "discriminatory conduct", but is coerced or induced to take unsafe action or to refrain from taking action for the promotion or support of work health and safety. The model WHS Act accordingly provides a prohibition against a person who organises or takes, or threatens to organise or take, any action against another person with intent to coerce or induce the other person or a third person to:

- exercise a power or not to exercise a power under the model WHS Act, or do so in a particular way (or propose to do so);
- perform a function in a particular way or not to perform a function (or propose to perform a function in a particular way or propose not to perform a function) under the model WHS Act; or
- refrain from seeking, or continuing to undertake, a role under the model WHS Act.

The model laws provide that, for the purposes of this prohibition, a reasonable direction given by an emergency services worker in an emergency is not an action with intent to coerce or induce a person.

The review Panel recommended that coercion should be found where the relevant action is taken without reasonable excuse. This element of recommendation 125 recognised that there may be circumstances where a person quite properly and reasonably persuades another to exercise a power, or not exercise a power, or do so in a particular way.[24] This has not been adopted in the model WHS Act. The proper exercise of the discretion of a regulator when deciding whether or not to prosecute, and of the court when determining whether to convict and/or impose a

---

24   See the discussion at para 29.47 of the Second Report. An HSR may be persuaded to not issue a provisional improvement notice, or direct a work stoppage, after being provided with facts by the PCBU.

penalty, will be critical to avoiding inappropriate and unjust consequences of this provision.

Prohibition of misrepresentation

A person must not knowingly or recklessly make a false or misleading representation to another person about that other person's:

- rights or obligations under the model WHS Act, or an instrument made under the Act;
- ability to initiate, or participate in, a process or proceedings under the model WHS Act, or an instrument made under the Act; or
- ability to make a complaint or enquiry to a person or body empowered under the model WHS Act to seek compliance with the Act or an instrument made under it.

This provision supports the prohibition of coercion or inducement.

Criminal proceedings for breach

A person who engages in or induces discriminatory conduct may be prosecuted for a breach of the model laws. In such proceedings, the burden of proving whether or not the conduct was undertaken for a prohibited reason is reversed. Where the prosecution proves that the relevant circumstances occurred (for example, taking action as an HSR) and adverse action was taken by the defendant against the person (for example, terminating or disciplining a worker), it is the defendant that must show that the prohibited reason was *not* the dominant reason for the conduct. That is, the defendant will need to prove that there was at least one other reason that was more significant or dominant than the prohibited reason.

A person will take action in relation to another for a reason. The person taking the action will know what that reason was, while others may only infer the reason from the circumstances. If a person has a proper, rather than a proscribed, reason for particular conduct, the person will present and support that reason. This is why the model WHS Act requires the person who acts to prove that a proscribed reason was not the dominant reason for doing so.

The model laws provide, in addition to a penalty, for a person who is convicted or found guilty of an offence to pay compensation to the victim of the discriminatory conduct or to employ, reinstate or re-employ that person to the relevant position (or, if it is not available, to a similar position).

Civil action

In addition to criminal proceedings for a breach, the model WHS Act provides for civil proceedings to be brought by a person who has been the subject of discriminatory conduct. As in criminal proceedings for discriminatory conduct, the defendant in civil proceedings will also have the burden of proof in relation to the reason for the conduct. In civil proceedings, however, the breach will be easier to prove, as the defendant must prove that the proscribed reason was not a *substantial* reason for the conduct. A substantial reason need not be the dominant one, but may be a lesser reason than others.

It will be a defence to civil proceedings if the defendant proves that the conduct was reasonable in the circumstances, *and* a substantial reason for the conduct was to comply with the model WHS Act or a corresponding work health and safety law.

A court may order a defendant to pay compensation to the person who was the subject of the discriminatory conduct, order that a worker be reinstated or re-employed in the same or a similar position, or that a prospective worker be employed. A court may order an injunction to restrain ongoing discrimination, or make "any other order that the court considers appropriate".

The model laws include provisions that prohibit multiple actions or "double-dipping". This is important, as the person who has been subjected to the discrimin-atory action may have rights of action under other laws relating to discrimination, including for "adverse action" under the *Fair Work Act 2009* (Cth).

How this differs from current laws

Occupational health and safety legislation in all jurisdictions currently provides for criminal offences for the types of discriminatory conduct contained in the model WHS Act. Some Acts provide for an order for compensation to be made on a finding of guilt, or allow civil action to be brought.

The model laws broaden the range of people who are protected by the prohibition against discriminatory conduct and broaden the proscribed reasons for the conduct. The WHS Act introduces offences for coercion and misrepresentation (which are similar to those found in the *Fair Work Act 2009* (Cth)[25]). The model laws also provide for civil action and remedies in all jurisdictions.

The test for finding whether the proscribed reason was a *dominant* one (criminal) or a *substantial* one (civil) differs from the standard that is currently applicable in some jurisdictions, and in some other laws.

Chapter

6

---

25 See *Fair Work Act 2009* (Cth), s 343 (coercion) and s 345 (misrepresentation).

CHAPTER 7

ENFORCEMENT AND COMPLIANCE

An obligation is meaningless if it is not enforced. Therefore, the enforcement and compliance provisions of the model Work Health and Safety Act (model WHS Act) are extremely important and, in very subtle ways, they change the approach to enforcement that is prevalent in most jurisdictions. From the treatment of the privilege against self-incrimination, to the enshrinement of legal professional privilege, to the accountability and liability measures in relation to the exercise of inspectors' powers, the model WHS Act places a new regime of enforcement and compliance on regulators and duty holders alike.

Parts 8 to 13 of the model WHS Act deal with enforcement and compliance. Parts 8 and 9 specify the role, functions and powers of the regulators, while Parts 10 to 13 deal with enforcement measures. This chapter explains these provisions in the context of the regime implemented by the model WHS Act.

Rationale for enforcement provisions

The model WHS Act contemplates an enforcement regime which promotes voluntary compliance but, through a graduated enforcement pyramid with criminal prosecution being the ultimate sanction, it is ultimately enforcement. This is reflected in the emphasis on enforcement options, such as enforceable undertakings.

The powers of enforcement are entrusted exclusively to the regulators. This was a contentious issue during the national review into model OHS laws because of the desire by the union movement to retain the power to prosecute (this power is currently available to unions in New South Wales and, since 2009, in the Australian Capital Territory).

In a sense, the model WHS Act retains and builds on the existing enforcement framework. Notice-based options are retained for lower-order enforcement activities, with enforcement powers graduating to prosecutions. A range of sentencing options are available to the courts following the conviction of a defendant (including injunctions and publicity orders).

The international context to this approach is provided in Australia's international obligations under ILO Convention 155[1] (a convention which Australia is a signatory to but has not yet ratified). Article 9 of that Convention provides:

> "1. The enforcement of laws and regulations concerning occupational safety and health and the working environment shall be secured by an adequate and appropriate system of inspection.
>
> 2. The enforcement system shall provide for adequate penalties for violations of the laws and regulations."

Article 10 requires measures to be taken to provide guidance to employers and workers so as to help them to comply with legal obligations.

Parts 8 and 9 of the model WHS Act give effect to article 9(1) of the ILO Convention by creating the role and functions of a regulator, and Parts 10 to 13 give effect to article 9(2) by creating an enforcement regime which is ultimately pursued through prosecutions as a last resort within an enforcement hierarchy.

In its deliberations, the Panel that undertook the national review into model OHS laws was at pains to emphasise the objective of voluntary compliance:

> "It is important that duty holders under the model Act have a clear understanding as to how they can comply with the legislation. While there will be provisions in the model Act focused on compliance and enforcement measures, the model Act should support an approach that seeks to gain voluntary compliance from duty holders."[2]

This approach, and indeed the approach of the model WHS Act, is consistent with the "enforcement pyramid" model of regulatory enforcement.[3]

Functions of the regulator

Although using model legislation for achieving harmonisation, each State and Territory will continue to have its own work health and safety regulator (that is, Comcare Federally, WorkCover in New South Wales and the Australian Capital Territory, Workplace Standards in Tasmania, Workplace Health and Safety in Queensland, and WorkSafe everywhere else). In an important step towards

---

1   International Labour Organization, *Occupation Safety and Health Convention, 1981* (no 155), Geneva, ILO, 1981.

2   Workplace Relations Ministers' Council, *National review into model occupational health and safety laws: second report to the Workplace Relations Ministers' Council* (Second Report), Canberra, WRMC, January 2009, p 251.

3   For a discussion of that model, see Gunningham, N and Johnstone, R, *Regulating workplace safety: systems and sanctions*, Oxford, Oxford University Press, 1999.

harmonising enforcement and compliance, the model WHS Act provides the framework for not only the powers, but also the role and functions, of these regulators.

The regulator has the following functions under the model WHS Act:[4]

- to advise and make recommendations to the Minister and report on the operation and effectiveness of the model WHS Act;
- to monitor and enforce compliance with the model WHS Act;
- to provide advice and information on work health and safety to duty holders under the model WHS Act and to the community;
- to collect, analyse and publish statistics relating to work health and safety;
- to foster a cooperative, consultative relationship between duty holders and the people to whom they owe duties and their representatives in relation to work health and safety matters;
- to promote and support education and training on matters relating to work health and safety;
- to engage in, promote and coordinate the sharing of information to achieve the objects of the model WHS Act, including the sharing of information with a corresponding regulator; and
- any other function conferred on it by the model WHS Act.

The regulator has the power to do all things necessary or convenient to be done for, or in connection with, the performance of the above functions. The regulator is also conferred all of the powers and functions that are conferred on an inspector under the model WHS Act. The regulator may delegate to any person (in writing) a power or function under the model WHS Act (other than the power of delegation).[5] The delegation may be made subject to conditions, is revocable, and does not derogate from the power of the regulator.

The regulator is also given powers to obtain information from a person where the regulator has reasonable grounds to believe that the person is capable of giving information or producing documents or records that give evidence in relation to a possible contravention of the model WHS Act or that will assist the regulator to monitor or enforce compliance with the model WHS Act.[6] This is an important extension of the regulator's powers in most jurisdictions in that it is not limited to an investigation of a contravention, but extends to ongoing compliance monitoring.

Chapter

7

---

4   Model WHS Act, s 151.
5   Model WHS Act, s 153.
6   Model WHS Act, s 154.

Incident notification

In practice, most prosecutions and many other enforcement activities are undertaken in response to an incident. As such, the incident notification provisions often act as the trigger for the enforcement pyramid. That is not to say that regulators do not undertake random inspections or pursue campaigns to emphasise an aspect of the legal obligations. They do this on a regular basis. But, by and large, most organisations will only come across a regulator after an incident. Under the model WHS Act, deaths, serious injuries or illnesses, and dangerous occurrences, are all notifiable incidents.[7]

What is a serious injury or illness?

Serious injury or illness is defined in the model WHS Act to mean an injury or illness requiring the person to have:

- immediate treatment as an in-patient in a hospital;
- immediate medical treatment for the amputation of any part of their body;
- immediate medical treatment for a serious head injury;
- immediate medical treatment for a serious eye injury;
- immediate medical treatment for a serious burn;
- immediate medical treatment for the separation of their skin from an underlying tissue (such as de-gloving or scalping);
- immediate medical treatment for a spinal injury;
- immediate medical treatment for the loss of a bodily function;
- immediate medical treatment for serious lacerations; or
- medical treatment within 48 hours of exposure to a substance.[8]

It is also anticipated that the regulations will prescribe additional injuries or illnesses that require notification.[9]

What is a dangerous incident?

The model WHS Act defines a dangerous incident as an incident in relation to a workplace that exposes a worker or any other person to a serious risk to a person's health or safety emanating from an immediate or imminent exposure to:

- an uncontrolled escape, spillage or leakage of a hazardous or potentially hazardous substance;

---

7   Model WHS Act, s 34.
8   Model WHS Act, s 35.
9   Note that s 34 of the model WHS Act permits certain injuries and illnesses to be prescribed as being excluded from notification.

- an uncontrolled implosion, explosion or fire;
- an uncontrolled escape of gas or steam;
- an uncontrolled escape of a pressurised substance;
- electric shock;
- the fall or release from a height of any plant, substance or object;
- the collapse, overturning, failure or malfunction of, or damage to, any plant that is required to be authorised for use in accordance with the regulations;
- the collapse or partial collapse of a structure;
- the collapse or failure of an excavation or of any shoring supporting an excavation;
- the inrush of water, mud or gas in workings in an underground excavation or tunnel; or
- the interruption of the main system of ventilation in an underground excavation or tunnel.[10]

It is anticipated that the regulations will prescribe additional incidents to the definition of dangerous incident.[11]

Who has the duty to notify?

The duty to notify incidents is imposed on a person who is conducting a business or an undertaking (PCBU) with respect to incidents arising from the conduct of the business or undertaking.[12] Since more than one person can be conducting a business or an undertaking at the same time, the duty to notify can, and will usually, fall on several people simultaneously. The notice must be given by the fastest means possible by telephone or in writing (including email, facsimile or other electronic means).

A person conducting a business or an undertaking must keep a record of the notification for at least five years.

Does a site have to be preserved?

The model WHS Act requires the site of a notifiable incident to be preserved until an inspector arrives or such earlier time as the inspector directs.[13] This is a shift away from the approach in some jurisdictions to limit the preservation power to more serious incidents. It also represents a shift away from the approach in some jurisdictions to have a time limitation on that obligation.

---

10   Model WHS Act, s 36.
11   Note that s 36 of the model WHS Act permits certain incidents to be prescribed as being excluded from the notification requirements.
12   Model WHS Act, s 37.
13   Model WHS Act, s 38.

Chapter

7

It is interesting to note that the obligation is qualified by reasonable practicability. The preservation of some sites is associated with significant opportunity costs (in terms of lost production or holding costs). How these competing components of the reasonably practicable qualification will be applied in practice in relation to site preservation remains to be seen. The duty, however, does not preclude steps taken:

- to assist an injured person;
- to remove a deceased person;
- that are essential to make the site safe or to minimise the risk of a further incident;
- that are associated with a police investigation; or
- for which an inspector or the regulator has given permission.

Who has the duty to preserve a site?

The duty to preserve a site is imposed on the person with the management or control of a workplace. However, there is no specific requirement for a PCBU to notify the person with the management or control of the workplace. That is, apart from the duty to consult and cooperate with other duty holders, a PCBU is under no obligation to do so.

It is also not clear whether the duty holder contemplated by the model laws is an individual employee or officer, or a corporate entity, or both. In choosing to refer to the person with the management or control of the workplace, rather than the PCBU to the extent that this includes the management or control of a workplace (the terminology of s 19 of the model WHS Act), it is arguable that the drafters intended the duty to fall on the employee or officer with that responsibility at the workplace, rather than the corporate entity that employs them. The policy rationale behind such a shift in approach is not entirely clear and was not recommended by the Panel.

Function of inspectors

The model WHS Act gives regulators the power to appoint inspectors, and specifies the minimum requirements for inspectors.[14] The regulators must issue inspectors with identification cards, and inspectors are required to produce their identification

---

14   Model WHS Act, s 155. These requirements are that the person must be: a public servant; an employee of a public authority; the holder of a statutory office; a person who is appointed as an inspector under a corresponding work health and safety law; or a person in a prescribed class of people. Section 157 of the model WHS Act prescribes a regime of disclosure of conflicts of interest by inspectors.

cards on request when exercising their powers. Identification cards must be returned if a person ceases to be an inspector.[15]

The model laws confer the following functions and powers on inspectors:[16]

- to provide information and advice about compliance with the model WHS Act;
- to assist in the resolution of work health and safety issues at workplaces;
- to assist in the resolution of issues related to access to a workplace by an assistant to a health and safety representative;
- to assist in the resolution of issues related to the exercise or purported exercise of a right of entry by a union;
- to review disputed provisional improvement notices;
- to require compliance with the model WHS Act through the issuing of notices;
- to investigate contraventions of the model WHS Act and assist in the prosecution of offences; and
- to attend coronial inquests in respect of work-related deaths and examine witnesses.[17]

In addition to these functions, inspectors have significant powers to enter workplaces and, on entry, to conduct investigations (including the collection of information and records).

Powers of inspectors

An inspector may, at any time, enter a place that is, or that the inspector reasonably suspects is, a workplace.[18] If, on entry, they discover that it is not a workplace, they are required to leave immediately.[19] The inspector is not required to give notice prior to entry, but must do so as soon as reasonably practicable. The notice needs to be given to:

---

15 Model WHS Act, s 156.

16 Model WHS Act, s 159.

17 An inspector's compliance powers are subject to any conditions or restrictions specified in the instrument of the inspector's appointment (model WHS Act, s 160). Furthermore, an inspector is subject to the regulator's directions in the performance of the inspector's compliance powers (model WHS Act, s 161).

18 Note the broad definition of workplace in s 8 of the model WHS Act (discussed in ch 4), and the limitations on the exercise of any powers in relation to residential premises in s 169 of the model WHS Act.

19 Note that an inspector may enter any place if the entry is authorised by a search warrant. They may also enter residential premises to gain access to a workplace.

- the person who is or appears to be in charge of the workplace;
- any person conducting a relevant business or undertaking at the workplace; and
- any health and safety representative for workers who is carrying out work for that business or undertaking at the workplace.

However, an inspector is not required to notify any person if to do so would defeat the purpose for which the place was entered or cause unreasonable delay.

On entry, the inspector has extremely broad powers.[20] They may:

- inspect, examine and make inquiries at the workplace;
- inspect and examine any thing (including a document or record) at the workplace;
- bring to the workplace, and use, any equipment or materials that may be required;
- take measurements, conduct tests and make sketches or recordings (including photographs, films, and audio, video, digital or other recordings);
- take and remove for analysis a sample of any substance or thing without paying for it;
- require a person at the workplace to give the inspector reasonable help to exercise the inspector's powers;
- exercise any compliance power or other power that is reasonably necessary to be exercised by the inspector for the purposes of the model WHS Act;
- require a person to tell the inspector who has custody of, or access to, a record or document;
- require a person who has custody of, or access to, a record or document to produce that record or document to the inspector while the inspector is at that workplace (or within a specified period);[21]
- require a person at the workplace to answer any questions posed by the inspector;[22]
- make copies of, or take extracts from, a record or document that has been given to the inspector in accordance with a requirement under the model WHS Act;

---

20   See the model WHS Act, s 164, 170, 173 and 174.

21   By written notice, unless the circumstances require the inspector to have immediate access to the record or document.

22   An interview conducted by an inspector must be conducted in private if the inspector considers it appropriate, or if the person being interviewed so requests. This does not limit the operation of s 165 of the model WHS Act or prevent a representative (for example, a lawyer) of the person being interviewed from being present at the interview.

- keep that record or document for the period that the inspector considers necessary;[23]
- seize any thing (including a document or record) at the place if the inspector reasonably believes that the thing is evidence of an offence against the model WHS Act; and
- take and remove for examination, analysis or testing a sample of any substance or thing without paying for it.[24]

When exercising their powers, an inspector is permitted to have a person assist them (including an interpreter).[25]

An inspector may require a person to provide their name and address if the inspector finds the person committing an offence against the model WHS Act or finds the person in suspicious circumstances.[26] An inspector is also permitted to attend and ask witnesses questions at coronial inquests into the deaths of workers.[27] The model WHS Act also makes provision for obtaining warrants to enter and search premises in in order to assist in the exercise of powers of enforcement under the Act.[28]

Legal professional privilege

Despite the scope of the powers of inspectors to seek information and demand the production of documents, the model WHS Act provides an express protection of communications (including documents) which are subject to legal professional privilege.[29]

Information and documents will be privileged if they were created for the dominant purpose of providing legal advice or in contemplation of legal proceedings. It is now common practice for organisations to engage lawyers to advise them in relation to their legal liability arising from an incident. It is also common practice for lawyers

---

23 While an inspector retains custody of a record or document, the inspector must permit the person who produced the record or document, and any person authorised by them, to inspect or make copies of the record or document at all reasonable times.
24 See s 174 of the model WHS Act in relation to restrictions on seizure where entry is gained with the consent of the occupier. See s 175 of the model WHS Act in relation to seizure of dangerous workplaces (or parts of workplaces). Note the broad definition of workplace and note that this may include a vehicle. Section 176 of the model WHS Act provides powers supporting seizure; s 177 of the model WHS Act requires the provision of a receipt in relation to any exercise of the power of seizure; and s 179 and 180 of the model WHS Act deal with the return of seized things and access to seized things, respectively.
25 Model WHS Act, s 165.
26 Model WHS Act, s 184.
27 Model WHS Act, s 186. Note the broad definition of worker.
28 Model WHS Act, s 166–168.
29 Model WHS Act, s 251.

to be engaged to conduct incident investigations because of their specialist investigative skills. Provided that the dominant purpose of such reports or advice is the provision of legal advice in relation to liability, those documents will be privileged. Regulators are used to claims of privilege in relation to properly commissioned investigation reports and legal advice.

Despite its prevalence, legal professional privilege is not well understood in the context of safety. It is often seen as a "trick", like a magic wand that you wave over documents. Or some sort of black magic that you should not engage in if you are "serious about safety". Neither is true.

Writing "privileged" on a document which is otherwise not privileged does not render it so. Conversely, failing to write it does not make it not privileged. An investigation report that has been prepared in compliance with a requirement of a corporate policy can never meet the dominant purpose test, since its dominant purpose will be compliance with the corporate policy — rather than the provision of legal advice.

On the other hand, the negative perception of the invocation of privilege is unwarranted. Safe organisations are organisations that investigate incidents in order to get to the root causes, that is, to uncover the system deficiencies and organisational factors that caused the absence or failure of defences or controls. However, by embarking on this inquiry, the organisation and its officers are exposed to significant penalties. By invoking a privileged investigation, the organisation can embark on the inquiry without fear of it unnecessarily incriminating the company.

The model WHS Act entrenches the legitimate role of privileged advice and investigations, and will go a long way to promoting acceptance of that approach.[30] If organisations use the privilege appropriately, it will lead to more thorough and confronting investigations and corrective actions.

Privilege against self-incrimination

One of the most significant reforms that the model WHS Act has made in relation to enforcement is the introduction of the privilege against self-incrimination. The right to silence is fundamental to the operation of the criminal law. However, some jurisdictions had abrogated that common law right in favour of a protection in relation to the use of the information gathered against the backdrop of the exercise of that privilege. Interestingly, this was not the approach recommended by the Panel. This will be a significant change in most jurisdictions.

---

30   Model WHS Act, s 251.

Under the model laws, a person is not excused from answering a question, or providing a document, a record or information, on the grounds that the answer to the question, or the document, record or information, may tend to incriminate the person or expose them to a penalty.[31] However, the answer to a question or a document, a record or information provided by an individual is not admissible as evidence against that individual in civil or criminal proceedings — other than proceedings arising out of the false or misleading nature of the answer, document, record or information.

Before a person is required to produce a document, a record or information or answer a question, an inspector must:

- identify themselves to the person as an inspector by producing the inspector's identity card (or in some other way);
- warn the person that failure to comply with the requirement or to answer the question, without reasonable excuse, would constitute an offence;
- warn the person about the effect of the abrogation of the privilege against self-incrimination; and
- advise the person about the protection afforded to documents which are privileged and confidential.

Liability in relation to damage

The model WHS Act seeks to make inspectors accountable for their conduct in relation to the exercise of their powers and functions in a way that is not usually seen in legislation of this kind. Under the model laws, an inspector is required to take all reasonable steps to ensure that they cause as little inconvenience, detriment and damage as is practicable in the exercise, or purported exercise, of a compliance power.[32]

Importantly, a person may claim compensation from the State if they incur loss or expense because of the exercise, or purported exercise, of the inspector's powers on entry to a workplace (including complying with a requirement made of the person). No restrictions are placed on what loss or expense may mean. For example, financial losses arising from the delays caused by an inspector exercising their powers may relevantly be a loss or an expense.

Compensation may be claimed and ordered in a proceeding that is brought in a court with jurisdiction for the recovery of the amount claimed, or for an offence against the model WHS Act which is brought against the person claiming compensation.

---

31   Model WHS Act, s 171.
32   Model WHS Act, s 181.

The court may order compensation to be paid only if it is satisfied that it is just to make the order in the circumstances of the particular case.[33]

Obstruction and impersonation offences

It is an offence to intentionally hinder or obstruct an inspector when they are exercising their compliance powers, or to induce or attempt to induce any other person to do so.[34] It is also an offence to directly or indirectly assault, threaten, intimidate, or attempt to assault, threaten or intimidate, an inspector or a person who is assisting an inspector,[35] and it is an offence to impersonate an inspector.[36]

Enforcement measures

Either through their inspectors or directly, a regulator has a range of enforcement options at their disposal, graduating from notices to prosecutions. They may:

- issue a non-disturbance notice;
- issue an improvement notice;
- issue a prohibition notice;
- take remedial action;
- obtain an injunction;
- enter into an enforceable undertaking;
- issue a penalty notice; and[37]
- initiate a prosecution for breach of the model WHS Act.

Non-disturbance notices

An inspector may issue a non-disturbance notice to the person with the management or control of a workplace if the inspector reasonably believes that it is necessary to do so to facilitate the exercise of their compliance powers.[38] It is an offence to fail to comply with a non-disturbance notice without reasonable excuse.[39]

---

33 The regulations may prescribe matters that may, or must, be taken into account by the court when considering whether it is just to make the order.

34 Model WHS Act, s 186.

35 Model WHS Act, s 189.

36 Model WHS Act, s 188.

37 Division 3 of the model WHS Act foreshadows the use of such notices but no details are available at this stage as the mechanism will depend on each of the jurisdictions. For this reason, this is not discussed further here.

38 Model WHS Act, s 197. Section 198 of the model WHS Act prescribes the minimum content of that notice; s 208 deals with service of notices; and Part 12 deals with the review of notices. Note that subsequent notices may be issued pursuant to s 200 of the model WHS Act.

39 Model WHS Act, s 199.

Improvement notice

If an inspector reasonably believes that a person is contravening or has contravened a provision of the model WHS Act in circumstances that make it likely that the contravention will continue, the inspector may issue an improvement notice requiring the person to:

- remedy the contravention;
- prevent a likely contravention from occurring; or
- remedy the things or operations that are causing the contravention or likely contravention.[40]

It is an offence to fail to comply with an improvement notice within the period specified in the notice.[41]

Prohibition notices

If an inspector reasonably believes that an activity is occurring, or may occur, at a workplace that involves, or will involve, a serious risk to the health or safety of a person (emanating from an immediate or imminent exposure to a hazard), the inspector may give a person who has control over the activity a direction prohibiting the carrying on of the activity, or the carrying on of the activity in a specified way, until the inspector is satisfied that the matters that give, or will give, rise to the risk have been remedied.[42] Failure to comply with a prohibition notice is an offence.[43]

Remedial action

If a prohibition notice is issued to a person and they fail to take reasonable steps to comply with the notice, the regulator may take any remedial action that it believes reasonable to make the workplace or situation safe (after giving written notice to the person to whom the prohibition notice was issued of the regulator's intention to take that action, and of the owner's or person's liability for the costs of that action).[44] The regulator may recover the costs of the remedial action from the person who failed to comply with the prohibition notice.[45]

---

40 Section 191 of the model WHS Act prescribes the minimum content of improvement notices; s 193 provides a mechanism for seeking an extension of time to comply with the notice; s 208 deals with service of notices; and Part 12 deals with the review of notices.
41 Model WHS Act, s 192.
42 Model WHS Act, s 194. Section 195 of the model WHS Act prescribes the minimum content of prohibition notices; s 208 deals with service of notices; and Part 12 deals with the review of notices.
43 Model WHS Act, s 196.
44 Model WHS Act, s 210.
45 Model WHS Act, s 212.

If the regulator reasonably believes that circumstances exist in which a prohibition notice can be issued and a prohibition notice cannot be issued at a workplace because, after taking reasonable steps, the person with the management or control of the workplace cannot be found, the regulator may take any remedial action that is necessary to make the workplace safe.[46] The regulator may recover the costs of taking that remedial action from the person on whom the notice would have been issued.[47]

Injunctions

As a further escalation measure, the regulator may apply to a court for an injunction that compels a person on whom a non-disturbance, improvement or prohibition notice has been issued to comply with the notice.[48] This is a new power that the model WHS Act has introduced. Because of the likely expense of such proceedings, it will no doubt be used sparingly. However, its availability gives the regulator addition options in the face of a recalcitrant duty holder.

Enforceable undertakings

The regulator may also accept a work health and safety undertaking in connection with the matter giving rise to a contravention of the model WHS Act as an alternative to prosecution.[49] Once accepted, no proceedings can be brought against the person in relation to the contravention giving rise to the undertaking. This is an initiative that has been in place for some time in most Australian jurisdictions. If appropriately administered, it has the potential to better achieve the objectives of the model WHS Act in that money is diverted from punitive action towards proactive compliance initiatives. Workplace Health and Safety Queensland is recognised for having administered its enforceable undertaking regime most effectively among its peer regulators.[50] As a result, a number of innovative initiatives have been undertaken under that regime which have benefited work health and safety. Enforceable undertakings are not available in relation to category 1 offences.

Importantly, the giving of an undertaking does not constitute an admission of guilt by the person who gives the undertaking. This has been a practical roadblock to at least one jurisdiction accepting the enforceable undertaking regime.

---

46   Model WHS Act, s 211.
47   Model WHS Act, s 212.
48   Model WHS Act, s 213–214.
49   Model WHS Act, s 215–221.
50   In the five-year period to mid-2008, there were 105 applications for such undertakings. Of these, 51% were accepted, 29% were rejected, and 21% were withdrawn. The average monetary value of an accepted undertaking was $178,000, which was five times greater than the average value of a court penalty ($34,000). The highest monetary value of an undertaking was $1.5m. In some cases, the value of the undertaking was over 30 times the highest available fine.

The regulator must give the person who is seeking to make an undertaking written notice of its decision to accept or reject the undertaking and of the reasons for its decision, and the regulator must publish, on its website, notice of its decision to accept an undertaking and the reasons for that decision. This is critical, as it promotes transparency and accountability in the system. It also promotes the option more generally as an alternative to prosecution.

An undertaking becomes enforceable when the regulator's decision to accept the undertaking is given to the person who made the undertaking or at any later date specified by the regulator.

It is an offence for a person to contravene an undertaking that has been given to the regulator.[51] In the event of a contravention, the regulator may commence proceedings for a breach and apply to the court for orders requiring the specific performance of the undertaking. The regulator may also commence proceedings in relation to the matters to which the undertaking related.

Legal proceedings

Prosecutions are the last resort in the hierarchy of enforcement powers and, being criminal in nature, they are not brought lightly. The power to commence prosecutions under the model WHS Act has been entrusted to the regulators only (either directly or through their inspectors).[52] The regulators are required to publish (on their website) guidelines for applying for an enforceable undertaking and for the circumstance where prosecutions will be commenced.

Review of decision not to prosecute

The model WHS Act contains a mechanism for review whereby the Director of Public Prosecutions can review a regulator's decision not to prosecute in relation to category 1 and 2 offences. The mechanism is based on a rarely-used section in the Victorian OHS legislation.[53]

If a person reasonably considers that the occurrence of an act, matter or thing constitutes a category 1 or 2 offence, and no prosecution has been brought in respect of the occurrence of the act, matter or thing after six months but not later than 12 months after that occurrence, they may write to the regulator requesting a prosecution to be brought. The regulator has three months to respond in writing to the person making the application and the alleged offender, and must give reasons why the prosecution will not be brought, if that is the decision made. The regulator must also advise the person making the application that they may ask for the matter

---

51 Model WHS Act, s 218.
52 Model WHS Act, s 229.
53 *Occupational Health and Safety Act 2004* (Vic), s 131.

to be referred to the Director of Public Prosecutions and, if directed to do so by the applicant, the regulator must refer the matter within one month of the request.

The Director of Public Prosecutions must consider the matter and advise (in writing) the regulator within one month as to whether the Director considers that a prosecution should be brought. The regulator must ensure that a copy of the advice is given to the person who made the request and the alleged offender. If the regulator declines to follow the advice of the Director of Public Prosecutions to bring proceedings, the regulator must give written reasons for its decision.

Limitation period

Proceedings for an offence under the model WHS Act must be brought within two years after the offence first comes to the notice of the regulator, and within one year after a finding in a coronial inquiry or an official inquiry that the offence has occurred. If the matter was the subject of an enforceable undertaking, proceedings must be brought within six months after the undertaking was contravened if it comes to the notice of the regulator that the undertaking has been contravened or the regulator has agreed to the withdrawal of the work health and safety undertaking.[54]

Sentencing options

The court has a wide range of options available to it in sentencing. It may:

- impose a penalty;
- make an adverse publicity order;
- make a restoration order;
- make a community service order;
- release the defendant on the giving of a court-ordered work health and safety undertaking;
- order an injunction; or
- make a training order.

Penalties

The model WHS Act provides a tiered regime of penalties, with the maximum penalty of $3m for a corporation and $600,000 and/or five years' imprisonment for individuals being reserved for the most serious breaches.

---

54 A proceeding for a category 1 offence may be brought after the end of the applicable limitation period if fresh evidence relevant to the offence is discovered, and if the court is satisfied that the evidence could not reasonably have been discovered within the relevant limitation period.

A person will be guilty of a category 1 offence if: they have a health and safety duty which they fail to comply with; without reasonable excuse, they engage in conduct that exposes an individual (to whom that duty is owed) to a risk of death or serious injury or illness; and they are reckless as to the risk of death or serious injury or illness to that individual. The maximum penalty for category 1 offences is $3m for corporations, $600,000 and/or five years' imprisonment for officers, and $300,000 and/or five years' imprisonment for workers. However, such offences are rare. They are associated with a high degree of culpability and, as such, the high penalty is warranted to reflect the community's disapproval of such conduct.

A person will be guilty of a category 2 offence if they have a health and safety duty which they fail to comply with, and the failure exposes an individual to a risk of death or serious injury or illness.[55] Category 2 offences attract a maximum penalty of $1.5m for corporations, $300,000 for officers, and $150,000 for workers.

All other offences are category 3 offences. They attract a maximum penalty of $500,000 for corporations, $100,000 for officers, and $50,000 for workers.

Adverse publicity orders

The court may make an order requiring an offender to publicise, in the way specified in the order, the offence, its consequences, the penalty imposed and any other related matter, and/or to notify a specified person or specified class of people, in the way specified in the order, of the offence, its consequences, the penalty imposed and any other related matter.

Offenders are required to give the regulator, within seven days after the end of the period specified in the order, evidence that the action or actions were taken by the offender in accordance with the order. The order can be made on the court's own initiative or on application.

If the offender fails to give evidence to the regulator of compliance with the order, the regulator, or a person authorised in writing by the regulator, may take the action or actions specified in the order. The regulator is entitled to claim the reasonable expenses associated with complying with the order in the offender's place.

Publicity orders have been available in OHS legislation for some time. On the whole, they have been used sparingly, much to the surprise of most commentators (given their potential).[56]

---

55 The Panel recommended that category 2 should apply where there is a serious risk of serious injury or death. The model WHS Act does not include the qualifier "serious".

56 See Tooma, M, *Tooma's annotated Occupational Health and Safety Act 2000 (NSW)* (3rd ed), Sydney, Thomson Reuters, 2009, pp 226–229, for a discussion of the publicity orders made in NSW under the *Occupational Health and Safety Act 2000* (NSW), s 115.

Restoration orders

The court may order an offender to take such steps to remedy any matter caused by the commission of the offence that appears to the court to be within the offender's power to remedy. The period for compliance may be extended by order of the court.

Community service orders

The court may make an order requiring the offender to undertake a specified project for the general improvement of work health and safety. The order may specify the condition associated with undertaking the project.

Court-ordered undertakings

The court may, without recording a conviction, adjourn the proceedings for a period of up to two years and make orders for the release of the offender on condition that the offender gives an undertaking to the court to comply with a specified condition. A court-ordered work health and safety undertaking must specify that:

- the offender appears before the court if called on to do so during the period of the adjournment and, if the court so specifies, at the time to which the further hearing is adjourned;
- the offender does not commit, during the period of the adjournment, any offence against the model WHS Act; and
- the offender observes any special conditions imposed by the court.

Injunctions

The court may issue an injunction requiring an offender to cease contravening the model WHS Act. This is a novel power which can be effective where penalty is not a real deterrent. For example, commercial imperatives may be the driver for continuing breaches of the model laws by an organisation, such that the maximum penalties available for the breaches may not be sufficient to deter the continuation of the breach. An injunction can be used in those circumstances to achieve compliance.

Training orders

The court may make an order requiring an offender to undertake, or arrange for one or more workers to undertake, a specified training course. This is another novel power which may be used for organisations in relation to training classes of employees, supervisors or officers, or with respect to convicted officers themselves.

INDEX

Page

Adverse publicity orders 111
Auditing and review 41

Business risks 34

Civil action
  discriminatory conduct 92
Coercion
  prohibition of 91
  protection against 89
Community service orders 112
Consultation 75
Contractors
  rights and duties 54
Court-ordered undertakings 112
Criminal proceedings
  discriminatory conduct 92

Damages
  inspector's liability 105
Dangerous incident 98
Discrimination
  protection against 89
Due diligence
  consideration of incidents,
    hazards and risks 39
  providing appropriate resources 35
Duty of care
  primary
    comparison with current
      OHS laws 27
    elements 24
    elements relating to specific
      activities of primary duty
      holders 26
    implications of new duties 28
    owing of duty 20
    rationale 16
    "reasonably practicable" 17
  officers 32
    acquisition of safety knowledge . . . 33
    auditing and review 41

Page

  consideration of incidents,
    hazards and risks 39
  existing regime 42
  legal compliance 40
  providing appropriate resources . . . 35
  rationale 29
  understanding business risks 34

Enforceable undertakings 108
Enforcement and compliance
  functions of regulator 96
  incident notification 98
  inspectors
    functions 100
    obstruction and impersonation
      offences 106
    powers 101
  legal professional privilege 103
  liability in relation to damage 105
  privilege against self-incrimination . 104
  rationale 95
  sentencing options 110

Harmonisation
  achieving consistency and
    improvement in OHS regulation . . . 9
  accommodating changed
    workplace arrangements 10
  aim to improve OHS regulation 12
  benefits 3
  brief history of work health and
    safety laws in Australia 1
  jurisdictional "uniqueness" 3
  national OHS review 5
  ongoing process 13
  ongoing review of legislation 2
  use of enforcement to achieve
    better safety outcomes 12
Health and safety committees 84
Home occupants
  rights and duties 54

Page

Horizontal engagement 73

Improvement notices 107
Incident notification. 98
Inducement
    prohibition 91
Injunctions. 112
    notices 108
Inspectors
    functions. 100
    improvement notices. 107
    liability in relation to damage 105
    non-disturbance notices 106
    obstruction and impersonation
        offences 106
    powers 101
    prohibition notices 107
    remedial action 107
Issue resolution. 78

Legal compliance 40
Legal proceedings. 109
Legal professional privilege. 103
Liability
    damage 105
    officers 64

Misrepresentation
    prohibition 92
    protection against 89

National OHS review. 5
Non-disturbance notices. 106

Officers
    duty of care. 32
        acquisition of safety
            knowledge 33
        auditing and review 41
        consideration of incidents,
            hazards and risks 39
        existing regime. 42
        legal compliance 40
        providing appropriate resources . . . 35
        rationale 29
        understanding business risks 34
    public sector liability. 64

Page

Participation and protection
    consultation, cooperation and
        coordination between duty
        holders. 72
    issue resolution 78
    protection against discrimination,
        misrepresentation and coercion . . . 89
    rationale 68
    union right of entry 85
    worker consultation 75
    worker representation 80
Penalties. 110
Person conducting a business or an
    undertaking (PCBU)
    consultation 68; 75
    primary duty of care 20
    protection against discrimination,
        misrepresentation and coercion . . . 71
    workers having same liability. 51
Prohibition notices. 107
Public sector obligations
    Act binds Crown. 61
    "Crown" 62
    liability of officers 64
    privilege against self-incrimination . . 63
    proceedings against successors to
        public authorities. 63

Regulator
    enforceable undertakings. 108
    functions. 96
    injunctions 108
    legal proceedings. 109
Representation 80
    determining 81
Restoration orders 112
Reviews
    decisions not to prosecute 109
Right of entry
    breaches 87
    powers 87
    qualifications for entitlement 85
    requirements and processes 76
    resolution of disputes 88
Rights and duties at workplaces
    workers and other people 53

Page

comparison of new and
    existing duties 53
duty of care 52
rationale 49
less liability than PCBU. 51
"person at workplace" 53
protection against victimisation. . . 56
"worker" 52
"workplace". 53

Safety performance reporting 34
Self-incrimination
    privileges against 63; 104
Sentencing options. 110
Serious injury or illness. 98
Shopping centre customers
    rights and duties 54

Training
    officers 33
    orders 112

Page

Union officials
    rights and duties 55
Unlawful discrimination. 90

Victimisation
    protection against 56
Volunteers
    rights and duties 54

Worker consultation — see Consultation
Worker representation — see Representation
Workplace participation and
    protection — see Participation and
    protection
Workplace rights and duties — see
    Rights and duties at workplaces